DATE DUE

DEMCO, INC. 38-3012

How to Create
INTERIORS
for the
DISABLED

The International Symbol of Access was adopted in 1969 to denote architectural accessibility in buildings and facilities usable by people with limited mobility.

How to Create
INTERIORS
for the
DISABLED

A Guidebook for Family and Friends

by **Jane Randolph Cary**

with a foreword by **Howard A. Rusk, M.D.,**
and **Sharon Wright**

Illustrations by Philip F. Farrell, Jr.

 PANTHEON BOOKS, New York

Library of Congress Cataloging in Publication Data

Cary, Jane Randolph.
    How to Create Interiors for the Disabled.

    Includes index.
    1.   Architecture and the physically handicapped.
I.   Title
NA2545.P5C37   728   77-88781
ISBN 0-394-41376-8
ISBN 0-394-73595-1 pbk.

Design by Irva Mandelbaum

Manufactured in the United States of America

First Edition

I see, Kiwi,
you have wings
but cannot fly.
Yes, that's true.
But what do you do?
Everything else.

Contents

Foreword

We've all heard it said at one time or another: "Necessity is the mother of invention." For the disabled and elderly, this saying should ring true, for there are times in each of their lives when something in or around their personal world becomes impossible to reach, manipulate, or otherwise operate. A person who has had a stroke encounters difficulty in getting up or down a flight of stairs; a young paraplegic can't raise a window because it sticks and is in front of a radiator; a quadriplegic is unable to get into, much less use, the suddenly too-small bathroom in his home because of a narrow doorway: these are just a few examples. They may seem like small annoyances, but for the disabled they can add up to more daily frustration than most people realize. A clever and resourceful friend or family member may be able to help make or find what is needed to solve the problem, but often this kind of help is not available.

The world of the disabled is frustrating enough without their home environment presenting extra difficulties that could so easily be remedied with a little thought and ingenuity. Yet in those hurried days before discharge from a rehabilitation center, neither the disabled person nor his family has time to think of everything. Moreover, harried rehabilitation specialists who are helping with the larger home-planning problems may overlook the many smaller solutions that would make each day a little more pleasant.

Jane Randolph Cary, in *How to Create Interiors for the Disabled*, has gathered together much useful information about techniques and equipment that can help solve a number of these problems. In her forthright presentation of problems and their solutions, Ms. Cary shows compassion and understanding not only for the disabled but for those who love and care for them. These friends and family members are often the ones to whom the task of getting a home ready to receive a disabled person falls, and they may be feeling equally anxious about what living at home again will be like. Too often, the feelings of these "caretakers" are bypassed in attempts to help or show concern for the disabled themselves.

This book should be especially helpful for those disabled individuals who have been patients in small rehabilitation centers that offered no home-planning guidance, or to whom no such centers were available. Too often eager hospital suppliers are most persuasive in selling hospital equipment to uninformed patients and families for home use when there is something equally safe and much more pleasant-looking that would fill the bill nicely. We wish we had a dime for every patient who has come into the Home Planning Unit at the Institute of Rehabilitation Medicine emphatically stating that he or she did not want us to help plan anything that would make the home look "institutional." We can quickly assure these patients that gray floors, pale green walls, and thick stainless steel grab bars do not have to be their only choice. Ms. Cary presents a cheerful, optimistic, yet realistic picture of what is available to us today for adapting the home environment.

But that is not the total picture. Once a home has been adapted and made comfortable, what about leaving it? That can be a scary thing to someone learning to cope with a disability. Here, too, Ms. Cary succeeds in giving an optimistic yet realistic view of the possibilities. Her candid discussions of life in the community, travel, the rights of the disabled, disabled consumer groups, and sources of information will all be most helpful to those who have been searching long and diligently. Learning that you are not alone is perhaps one of the most important points here. Though you may feel at the moment that your world has crashed in on you, others have been there, have shared some of the problems, and have worked out solutions that can benefit others in turn.

We have not yet reached utopia—one eye-blink will not turn on the morning coffee, bring in the paper from the porch, open it for you, turn its pages, or put the dishes in the dishwasher. But researchers are working on hitherto undreamed-of ways to improve the quality of life for the disabled. Their work creates prototypes that are turned into production-line items ready for the market, where they are within financial reach of more people. For now, making daily home life more than tolerable means scouring the market for those simple and fairly inexpensive items that were themselves expensive prototypes yesterday. *How to Create Interiors for the Disabled* brings us up to date on what is out there and how we can go about using it to create both a physical and a mental environment that the disabled person, as well as his family and friends, will want to come home to.

Howard A. Rusk, M.D.
Director
Institute of Rehabilitation Medicine

Sharon Wright, M.A.
Home Planning Consultant
Institute of Rehabilitation Medicine

Preface

Dear Reader . . .

Until four years ago, it seemed to me the active daily living needs of the disabled could be and were being satisfied by business, industry, and modern science. I was confident this was so because I had encountered so few mobility-impaired children and adults in my travels and had heard and read even less about them.

Moreover, I had no knowledge of how many physically disabled people there were among us. Other than the war-injured, how many more disabled could there be? Were we not already rushing at spaceship speed toward the heart of dazzling technological achievement? Were we not an inventive, resourceful, productive nation making more goods and services than we could use? In such an atmosphere of challenge and know-how, could there be much more left undone, unplanned?

Yes, I discovered there was. Lots more. In 1973, while scouting for a magazine article, I met a family who had just spent eighteen frustrating months trying to learn how best to build and furnish an addition to their home for their young daughter disabled by *spina bifida,* a congenital defect in the vertebrae. From them, I found out how difficult it is for people such as you, on your own, to equip, build, or modify a room, a house, an apartment for someone who uses crutches, canes, braces, prostheses, or a wheelchair.

From a medical point of view, rehabilitation medicine was responding to patients' needs—and, to some extent, families' needs—in an efficient and well-organized way. But once treated and trained, the disabled had no efficient and well-organized place to go except home to an environment that no longer fitted their bodies, or to institutions that no longer suited their need for self-fulfilling independence.

Astounding, but there it was: the entire subject of the physically disabled had been left untouched except by the relatively few men and women devoted to rehabilitation medicine and by the members of paralyzed veterans' organizations.

Somewhere in the forest long ago, a door closed while houses, villages, and systems of government were being shaped by the nondisabled for the nondisabled. Yet it must have been obvious to our leaders that the ranks of the disabled increased as the population increased; as wars continued apace; as assaults upon the environment grew more frenzied; as malevolent microbes became resistant to vaccines.

One wonders just how long the decision-makers thought the closed door would resist the pressures building up behind it. With no advance warning, that barrier crashed off its hinges in the spring of 1977. The disabled emerged, shouting, "We're here!"

And so they were—millions of them. The permanently disabled. The temporarily injured. The aging. All with specialized demands upon a system of practices and attitudes as yet unprepared to serve them. Nevertheless, they are marching, rallying, demonstrating for their rights to dignity, recognition, understanding, and above all, independence to live, work, and play as they choose.

This book is about the men, women, and children disabled by limited mobility, a physical impairment with no age, sex, race, or socioeconomic boundaries. It can affect young, old, and all in between. It can be caused by accident or illness. It can be severely limiting or only slightly so. It can happen gradually or suddenly.

Although this book is about the disabled, it is *for* the nondisabled: the family and friends who must do whatever they can, with whatever resources they have, to make everyday places more comfortable, more accessible to the one who is disabled.

While doctors and therapists strive to do all they can for their patients, their treatment and training techniques can do only so much; the environment has to give a little, too. At present, all the research and money that will help provide smoother passage into the mainstream is being spent to make the impersonal public sector more accessible to the disabled. And while experts in the fields of design, building, and social services continue talking with each other about what to do and how to do it, some very important questions in another area are going unanswered. What about the millions of private houses and apartments that need to be modified to accommodate the disabled? What about you who have or feel the responsibility for helping the disabled settle into new ways of living and working? Where do you go for remodeling or building advice? Where do you shop for products that will make it easier for the disabled to open a door, fry an egg, take a bath?

Ironically, unbelievably, in this continent-sized storehouse of abundance and specialization there are no well-marked routes for you to follow, no clearly defined sources for products or assistance.

Surely this oversight will be corrected soon. Meanwhile, the ideas you'll find in the pages that follow are offered to help relieve some of the confusion and burdensome trial-and-error you are trying to cope with now.

If the suggestions seem to be an odd combination of the primitive and the contemporary, I make no apologies, for they reflect circumstances as they are: the need to resort to Robinson Crusoe survival methods in a nuclear age. They also represent what the disabled have learned so well: to make do with what they have, what they can find, in whatever way they can.

Since this was not intended as a medical text or a technical handbook on construction methods, I conducted my research by talking with and visiting the disabled in their homes. I needed to see and understand how they adapted the spaces and objects around them to meet their personal needs. I found them willing, even eager, to share their ideas with me so I could pass them on to you. The doctors and therapists I consulted were cooperative and helpful, also, and understood that I was preparing a practical guide to handling some of the problems you are likely to encounter.

Some of the suggestions will work for you; others will not. I've attempted to give you a number of ideas from which you can choose whatever best suits your particular situation, adapt it as you wish, or be motivated to create something better.

You will find dimensions expressed in both standard and metric quantities. This makes the reading of measurements more difficult, since the system is unfamiliar. Moreover, a double set of numbers that designate one measurement will seem an unnecessary interruption in the usual flow of words and digits. To avoid confusion and irritation, you could consider underlining the standard quantities and blocking out the metric. But use pencil marks that can be erased later, for metric is on the way—to stay.

Names and addresses of manufacturers, distributors, and stores and the prices of products mentioned here are current as of July 1977. Taxes and charges for shipping and handling are not included.

Where large groups of related products are discussed—grab bars and plumbing fixtures, for instance—you will not find lists of prices, but rather the sources from which to order catalogues. These will usually contain a complete range of the items you're interested in, as well as other useful products you may not have known about otherwise. Shopping from catalogues will save you time and energy—two valuable resources which, if wisely conserved, will allow you to give some to the disabled child or adult in your life and reserve enough for someone else very important: yourself.

J.R.C.

New York,
August 1977

Acknowledgments

To the men, women, and children who allowed me to meet and know them while preparing this book, I am profoundly grateful. From their welcome came insight into experiences rarely glimpsed; from their candor appeared both the hard and soft edges of truths few of us have the opportunity to learn.

My deepest appreciation to Julia Schechter, Frances Lyons Barish, Betty Graliker, Chris O'Donoghue, Mary and Bill Walker, Dorothy and Jim Liston, and Claire and Al Scholz for inviting me into their homes; for sharing and confiding.

I am indebted to the doctors and therapists who patiently gave of their time and expertise, especially Dorothy Milner, O.T.R., and Sharon Wright, M.A., of the Institute of Rehabilitation Medicine, New York University Medical Center, who were not only helpful but tolerated my interruptions with kindness.

For the encouragement and enthusiastic support of Betts, Madelaine, Ruth, Gil, Nell, Bill, Margaret, Julia, Tish and Joe Sage, and Laughlin Rock, I wish this to tell them of my appreciation.

To the manufacturers and retailers who understood my quest and assisted me in it, my gratitude.

Special thanks go to Barbara Plumb, my editor, and to Phyllis Benjamin for their patient understanding and guidance of this project from beginning to end. And for designer Irva Mandelbaum's sensitivity and discerning eye, I am most grateful.

To Siew Thye Stinson go my personal thanks for her invaluable assistance with the manuscript, as well as for her constant support during trials only she and I know of.

And to Dr. Alice Loomer, whose wit, knowledge, courage, and generous spirit contributed more to me and this book than words can fully express, my warmest regards and deepest gratitude.

How to Create
INTERIORS
for the
DISABLED

Chapter 1

A Place of Their Own

Accessibility is a fighting word, these days. For two centuries, disabled Americans kept quiet about not being able to get into and out of buildings, use buses, trains, and planes, go to work, be entertained, have an education. But they will not be unheard, or unseen, any longer.

Suddenly, or so it seems to the nondisabled in this spring of 1977, the disabled are angry. They are banding together in public places, demanding their right to come and go wherever they want just like anyone else.

Their initial attacks are aimed at buildings and services supported in whole or in part by public funds; the disabled pay taxes, too. They recognize that it will be some time before the goals of accessibility are fully achieved, but at least now they know they can break down barriers, even bureaucratic ones.

Having or winning access to viable, independent lives as residents in their own houses and apartments is another matter, however.

Traditionally, the disabled are considered customers of the medical-institutional-commercial market, which makes purchases for them. Insofar as they live outside this supportive framework as average consumers, many of the goods and services they need are not available to them, or you, in the open market. Consequently, shaping and equipping a property to fit their individual needs is an exercise in ingenuity, a task the disabled are becoming quite good at and are asking you to share.

Even before they leave hospitals and treatment centers, the disabled are planning and being trained to live independently, relying on their own will power and the techniques of rehabilitation medicine to make it possible . . . and depending upon you, their family and friends, to make it happen.

But do you know what to do? Do you know how to reshape houses, rooms, and objects for someone with limited mobility?

There's no way you could know. No magic potion is going to endow you suddenly with the knowledge, the experience, the insight needed to modify the environment for this child or adult you care about. Even medical and building experts will tell you there's no universal blueprint to follow, that each disabled person's needs have to be met individually. But you want to help, and will try. Right now, you're wondering where to start.

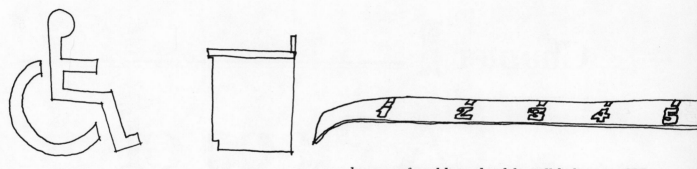

Follow the Dimensions

You begin by becoming familiar with a list of access guidelines formulated for architects, designers, and other professionals who are trying to make buildings fit people better. These specifications are based on averages, hence don't take individual differences into account. Furthermore, they are based on and formulated for public structures. But they do spring from one common denominator—the wheelchair—and are used to establish basic design requirements for making buildings (and things) accessible to the disabled. Also, anyone using crutches, braces, prostheses, or canes can maneuver within these boundaries.

The information on page 5 on the sizes of wheelchairs and the amount of room they and their occupants need to move from place to place comfortably and safely will help you plan an accessible home for your friend or relative.

Children's wheelchairs are smaller, of course, and are often used by adults who prefer the extra flexibility the reduced size offers in getting around corners and through doorways. For your own purposes, though, it would be wise to know in advance the size of the chair that's likely to be prescribed for your child and to carry a list of its dimensions with you. Ask the doctor or therapist to give you the measurements or else tell you how to go about getting them.

How Far Is Up?

Depending upon the disability, adults and children seated in wheelchairs have a range of reach that helps determine how well they can

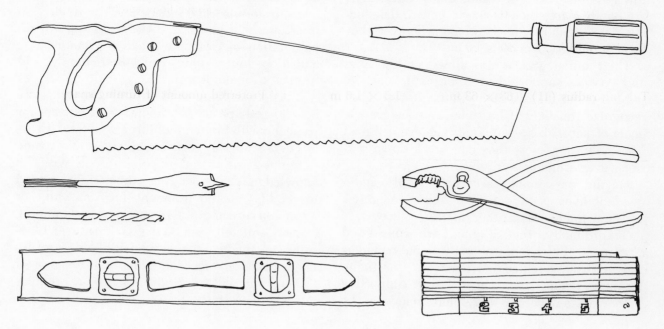

Adult Wheelchair	Standard	Metric	Notes
Length	42 to 44 in.	1,067 to 1,118 mm	Unoccupied but with footrests attached
Length	Add 4 to 6 in.	Add 102 to 152 mm	With adult occupant
Width	22½ to 26½ in.	572 to 873 mm	Unoccupied
Width	Add 4 to 6 in.	Add 102 to 152 mm	Occupied, allows for hands and elbows
Width	9 to 14½ in.	279 to 368 mm	Average folded width is 11 in./279 mm
Seat height	19½ in.	495 mm	Average above-floor height
Seat depth	16 in.	406 mm	Front-to-back measurement
Arm height	29½ in.	749 mm	Average above-floor height
Over-all height	36 in.	914 mm	Average above-floor height
Turning radius (I)	60 × 60 in.	1.5 × 1.5 m	Makes for tight full-circle turns, but OK
Turning radius (II)	63 × 63 in.	1.6 × 1.6 m	Preferred amount of turning space. What a difference 3 in./76 mm make!

function independently. The reach chart on page 6 will give you a good idea of how to arrange spaces and place objects that must be handled from a seated position.

A child's reach changes as he or she grows and develops new strengths. That's why a chart of averages wouldn't be much help. Your best bet is to ask the doctor or therapist, at each time of evaluation, to measure how far your child can reach. You can also measure it yourself as the youngster becomes more active at home.

Be very sensitive to how far a child can and

Direction of Adult Reach (seated)	Standard	Metric	Notes
Vertical	54 to 78 in.	1.4 to 1.9 m	Average is 60 in./1.5 m
Horizontal (I)	28½ to 33½ in.	724 to 851 mm	One arm extended
Horizontal (II)	54 to 71 in.	1.4 to 1.8 m	Both arms outstretched
Diagonal	48 in. above floor	1.2 m above floor	One arm extended toward shelf or wall

cannot reach. A delicate balance exists between beneficial challenge, which forces the child to extend, to develop a bit more power in order to reach what he wants, and outright frustration, which makes the child feel that no matter how hard he tries he will not succeed.

You may have to adjust the heights and widths of things in the house several times before everyone settles on what's best. So at first, keep the environment and your own feelings flexible; be ready to move a hook or raise a shelf from time to time.

Another group of dimensional requirements that will help you judge how to reshape and modify an independent-living environment are those gleaned from the Department of Health, Education, and Welfare handbook *Design of Barrier-Free Facilities* (Part 4, Series 4.12). These also are a set of impersonal-sounding statistics prepared by and for professionals, but as a guide they are useful. Besides, there isn't anything else. They are listed in this chapter (pages 9-11) as a kind of centralized information source, but will appear separately in related-subject chapters.

Right now, it's time to consider the differences involved in judging the accessibility of houses and apartments.

An apartment (whether owned, rented, or being shopped for) must be evaluated in terms of the building it's in, the surrounding neighborhood, and the attitude of building management and staff toward a disabled resident.

A house (whether owned, rented, or being shopped for) must be judged in relation to the property it's on and the neighborhood it's in.

Your job is to create a workable habitat in relation to the person's limitations and potentialities. You learn what these are from doctors, therapists, and others on the rehabilitation team at evaluation meetings prior to the person's release from the treatment center or hospital. (What you and the disabled need to know, and have the right to know, is covered in the next chapter.) But whatever kind of shelter your disabled friend or relative expects to return to, you'll be relieved to learn that modifying it will not be as complicated, extensive, or costly as you're imagining it to be.

The House

Just about the only places where altered shapes work better for the disabled than for the nondisabled are on stairs and in kitchens and bathrooms. What's more, few of the needed changes will detract from the appearance or re-sale value of the house. In fact, many of them are assets.

A wide roll-in shower, for example, is a joy to use and, compared with the confinement of conventional stalls, is an outright luxury. Electronically activated garage doors and exterior lighting are selling points all realtors appreciate. Additions such as wooden ramps are easy enough to dismantle and so should not deter a prospective buyer, although, before you have one removed, you might remind the prospective buyer that a ramp is a great time-and-energy-saver on moving day.

Plan on Paper First

So that you can arrange and budget for whatever remodeling has to be done, make a sketch, with dimensions, of the house and property. Make copies for the rehabilitation team, too; with these they can better advise you and train their patient for living at home. Use two sheets of paper, 8½ × 11 in./216 × 279 mm. On one, show the floor plan of the house; on the other, indicate how the house is situated on the property (simply show the house in outline), allowing room to note position, size, and distances of sidewalks, curbs, steps, porches, driveway, and the like.

In your sketch of the floor plan, show how wide the doorways are and the direction in which each door swings.

All this sounds exhausting, but it really isn't. You don't have to be an artist; all you are doing is jotting down a group of measurements over a rough sketch. Friends might even do the whole thing for you. They've probably been wanting to help you and the disabled, but were too upset or shy to ask. Just remember, the drawing doesn't have to win prizes, but the measuring has to be as accurate as possible because, where wheelchairs are involved, tiny bits of space do count.

•

Contractors and Building Codes

Once you and the rehabilitation team decide upon the best way to reshape the house and property, you can decide whether to do the job yourself or have someone else do all or part of the work. Either way, be sure you know what the local building codes and zoning regulations are before you begin a project. You don't want to find out after you've built a ramp, for instance, that it's illegal for one reason or another.

Finding contractors is easy but getting one to take the job is something else. Many are aware of the technical requirements for building for the disabled, but few have taken the time to learn the details. They may turn you down at once, or else take the job and attempt to do it their way. So shop for contractors by phone first, to save time, and make it clear that you know about slope requirements for ramps and the proper height for everything from door-knobs to plumbing fixtures.

Be willing and prepared to work along with anyone you hire, or else to supervise the work closely. This good advice comes from Al and Claire Scholz, who've begun reshaping their bungalow home since Claire has been confined to a wheelchair due to multiple sclerosis. Al, a good Sunday carpenter, is doing most of the work himself but needs to call in professionals from time to time. He warns that no matter how qualified and conscientious they are, they often don't listen; they hear you, but nine times out of ten they will do what they're most used to doing, which isn't always what you've asked for.

To avoid being sorry later, get a written contract detailing what is to be done, how, and with what materials; include the date the job is to begin, the date it's to be completed, and the total price and terms.

Shop for the best home-improvement loan you can find. As yet, there are no special loans or tax benefits available to private homeowners, unless they happen to be veterans. A qualified (disabled) veteran can apply for financial assistance under the terms offered by the Veterans Administration's Wheelchair 702 Housing provision. For information, call the VA office in which the veteran's claim records are filed. Other sources for legal and financial help are collected in Chapter 15.

If the House Is Rented

Some landlords are compassionate and understanding. Others are not. If the house, grounds, and neighborhood are valuable to the disabled person's sense of belonging and independence, then it's worthwhile finding out if the owner will let you modify his property.

Call to ask for an appointment. Approach him calmly and discuss the alterations you and the rehab team have decided are needed. In many instances, this may involve one entry ramp, or handrails, outside the house, and one or two wider doorways inside. Even if you need more than that—a bathroom on the first floor, for example—ask him to consider it, at least. A second bath can be a valuable asset to his property. If you can afford it, offer to pay for the work, or share a portion of the expenses. If you honestly do not have the money, say so; the owner still may be willing to help. And you'll never know unless you ask.

In case you are lucky enough to have or find a cooperative landlord, you'd be wise to have the new arrangements clearly spelled out in a lease.

If the owner turns out to be the negative variety, then it's time to shop for a new landlord. Here's where friends can help. Let them make calls and visit properties listed in the real estate pages of local newspapers. Supply them with a folding ruler or metal tape and a list of the dimensions a house or apartment should have in order to be accessible in terms of the disabled person's needs. Having someone else do the initial running around will relieve you of the pressures and worries you're now trying to cope with.

The Apartment

For the disabled, apartments have advantages that houses do not: proximity to shopping, transportation, and entertainment when they want it; elevators to lift them above it all when they don't. Even in small towns and suburban areas, where some of these features don't exist, there is still the convenience of having living room, bedroom, bath, and kitchen on one level. Indeed, a one-room apartment at ground level or in an elevator building might offer better opportunities for an independent life-style than a house; it certainly is a better alternative than being imprisoned in a larger apartment on the upper floor of a nonelevator building.

What to Look For

If an apartment building isn't accessible, then the apartment inside it is useless, no matter how well equipped. Look for a building with a direct level approach from public sidewalk or driveway. If there is a garage in the building, and the disabled person plans to use it, it should be served by an elevator with a floor-level approach.

Lobbies should be flush with the entryway, and elevators should be level with the lobby.

Elevators have to be a certain size, too, if they are to be used by someone in a wheelchair. The inside of the elevator cab should be at least 5 ft./1.5 m square, or 63 × 56 in./1.6 × 1.4 m; have call buttons that are easy to reach—centered at 42 in./1.1 m above the floor—and an emergency telephone no higher than 48 in./1.2 m above floor level. The opening into the elevator should be at least 32 in./813 mm wide.

Wheelchair users can't use revolving doors, so if the building you are judging has one, check to see if there is a swing-open or sliding door nearby which opens directly into the lobby.

In many buildings, the lobby is separated from the street by a foyer or vestibule, each with its own set of doors. If the two sets of doors swing toward each other, you may have a problem. As Figure 1–1 shows, there has to be at least 6 ft./1.8 m between the arcs of swing; otherwise a wheelchair user cannot manage to get through both sets of doors. If both sets of doors swing in the same direction, the problem is reduced; all that remains is the nuisance of having to handle two sets of doors, which are usually heavy ones.

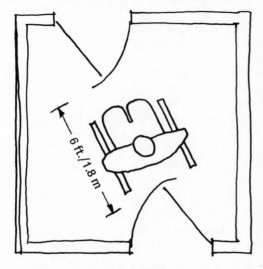

1–1 Distance between open vestibule doors must be 6 ft./1.8 m or more.

But if a building has doormen, a full-time service crew, or a superintendent, you're in luck, for almost nothing is as valuable to a disabled tenant as the help and understanding that can come from a sympathetic, cooperative staff. In addition to opening and closing doors, willing employees can make repairs, take messages, deliver mail, and run errands (when off duty). They can be an alert, protective link between the disabled and his or her family and friends, the police, the fire department—the world.

They can do these things and will . . . if their efforts are not taken for granted. Building employees are not required to work as civil engineers, social workers, psychologists, paramedics, or weight lifters. If they were, their salaries would reflect it.

The desire to help others cannot be bought, but it can be rewarded, and should be. Therefore, in arranging for an apartment for a disabled person, enlist the good will of the staff. Make it clear that their cooperation will be compensated; then make sure the promise is kept. You can also encourage a few friends and relatives to give the building staff cash gifts at Christmas in the name of the disabled tenant.

Think of this as a pay-off if you will, but bear this in mind: custodial care in an institution for a person who is or can be trained to be self-sufficient will cost nearly five times as much per month as a one- or two-room apartment in a full-service building. Even with a day-care attendant, such an arrangement would be less costly than an institution or "home."

Measurements That Matter

Inside a house or apartment are the rooms, doorways, hallways, fixtures, furnishings, and equipment designed and constructed according to time-honored specifications that are meant to accommodate strong, fully coordinated adults of average height. Some but not all of these spaces and objects work well for people with limited mobility; others have to be modified in various ways for the disabled to feel, and be, self-sufficient. Clues to how well a disabled child or adult can function at home are the dimensional requirements listed below. Use them as a guide in judging how accessible an existing or new habitat will be for your friend or relative.

Doors and doorways should have flush sills and a clear opening that is 32 in./813 mm wide. Doorknobs should be 36 in./914 mm above floor level.

A wheelchair user needs at least 24 in./610 mm of space at the side of an in-swinging door in order to be able to open it from a seated position (see Figure 1–3).

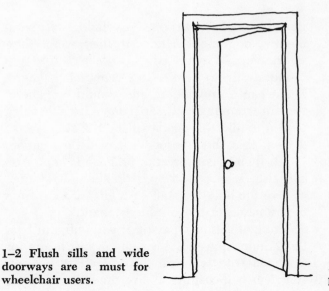

1–2 Flush sills and wide doorways are a must for wheelchair users.

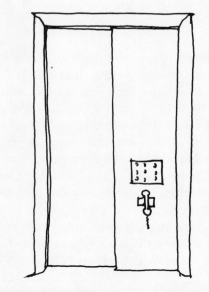

1–2A Make sure elevator doors open wide for smooth passage by wheelchair.

Handrails on steps and ramps should be 32 in./813 mm above the top surface for adults, 16 to 18 in./406 to 457 mm for children.

Hallways are tricky for the nondisabled to judge, so don't trust your eye. Measure accurately with a folding ruler or metal tape and keep these points in mind: a hallway has to be 48 in./1.2 m wide for an adult in a wheelchair to make a right-angle turn or move through doorways opening from it. However, in most houses and apartments, interior halls are 36 in./914 mm wide or less. While this presents some problems, there are ways to handle them. For instance, an extra-long or extra-wide chair cannot make a right-angle turn in such a hallway, but a small chair can. If the house is ideal for independent living in other ways, let the doctor or rehabilitation team know how wide the hallway is; they may be able to prescribe a chair that suits both the person and the house.

A chair turning from a 36 in./914 mm hallway cannot get through a doorway that's 27 in./686 mm wide, but if you remove the doorsill and widen the

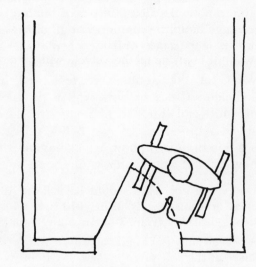

1–3 Allow 2 ft./610 mm of space at side of an inward-opening door.

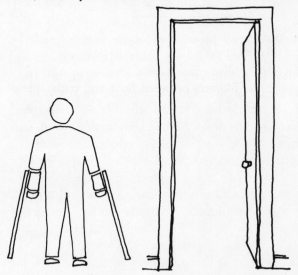

1–3A Crutch users also welcome wide doorways, flush sills.

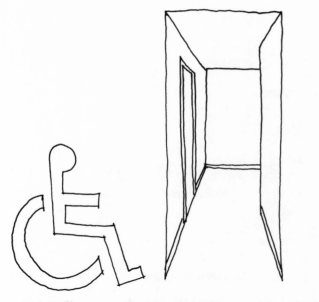

1–4 Hallways with right-angle turns must be wide; measure, don't guess.

opening to 36 in./914 mm, it can. Often it's far simpler to widen one or two doorways than to move to another home or opt for the long-term expense of institutional care.

Window sills should not be over 36 in./914 mm above the floor; otherwise a person seated in a wheelchair will not be able to see out.

Light switches should be 36 in./914 mm above the floor. Wall outlets should be no less than 18 in./457 mm above the floor; for people with small bodies, an outlet that's 24 in./610 mm above floor level would be even better. Fuse boxes should be 36 in./914 mm above the floor and placed so they are not blocked by furniture or other equipment.

Work surfaces, such as tables, desks, kitchen sinks, and bathroom lavatories, should be 32 in./813 mm above floor level, and have a knee-space clearance of 29½ in./749 mm between floor and underside of the surface. This means that bracings, aprons, or fascias usually used as supports for the top have to be cut out, made smaller than usual, or eliminated altogether.

Built-in wall ovens should be mounted so that the bottom of the oven door is 29½ in./749 mm above floor level.

Base cabinets should have a work surface that is 32 in./813 mm above the floor and have a bigger-than-usual toe space: 9 in./229 mm high and 6 in./152 mm deep. This extra-large recess at the bottom of the cabinet allows a wheelchair user to get closer to the counter.

Bathrooms should have a clear floor space of 60 × 60 in./1.5 × 1.5 m to allow a wheelchair to turn around in it. Grab bars and towel bars should be securely fastened to the walls and be 33 in./838 mm above the floor. Mirrors, shelves, and medicine cabinets should be set quite low: from 30 in./762 mm to no higher than 40 in./1,016 mm.

Hanging rods in clothes closets should be no higher than 48 in./1.2 m above the floor for most adults and 30 to 36 in./762 to 914 mm high for small people and children.

Beds should be raised on blocks or lowered so that the top surface of the mattress is level with the seat of the wheelchair; then a person can slide from one onto the other.

Sofas and chairs with seats 18 in./457 mm above floor level are ideal for the elderly and those who use crutches, canes, or braces.

Outside spaces have to be considered, too, especially if the person is active—or determined to become so. Sidewalks should be from 36 to 48 in./914 mm to 1.2 m wide. They should be smooth but not slippery, and be at the same level as the ground on both sides, or else have bumpers, low guardrails, or handrails on both sides. If they cannot be absolutely flat, they must be gently sloped; see the slope chart for ramps on page 20 for guidelines.

Parking space for a car or van has to be wide enough for the disabled person to transfer from chair or crutches to vehicle and vice versa. Usually a firm, level space of from 4 to 5 ft./1.2 to 1.5 m wide at one side of the vehicle will be ample.

Firm Fastenings

How many times have you grabbed a towel bar to keep from slipping, or used it to brace yourself against when changing a light bulb or reaching for something? Plenty of times, probably; it is after all handy, and if you're lucky, it hasn't given way under you. But towel bars are no substitute for safety grab bars, and the disabled will use anything that's nearby to lever and haul themselves around; not just some of the time but all the time. Therefore, be sure to anchor all rods, racks, bars, and shelves firmly by using the fastener that is best suited for the kind of wall involved.

For hollow walls use toggle (or wing) bolts or else molly (or mushroom) bolts, although if the bar, rack, or shelf is likely to be subjected to a lot of pulling or pressure, choose toggle bolts; they are better able to take the wear and tear.

Use expansion bolts in solid masonry walls. These bolts are sometimes called anchors, or plugs; they come complete with screws of appropriate size.

If you plan to fasten anything to a wood stud, or it just happens that way, use wood screws.

Manufacturers of safety grab bars are anxious that their product be mounted properly, and so have carefully prepared installation instructions for all types of walls; follow their directions carefully.

Anchor bolt with screw

Masonry

1–6 Fastener for masonry walls.

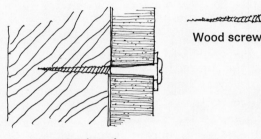

Wood screw

Wood stud

1–7 Fastener for wood studs and walls.

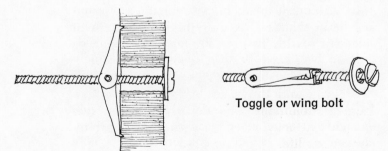

Toggle or wing bolt

Plaster

Molly or mushroom bolt

Sheetrock

1–5 Fasteners for hollow walls.

Chapter 2

Your Right to Know

Whether the disability now affecting the child or adult in your life occurred suddenly or gradually, you cannot be expected to know how to handle the injured person's needs and feelings (or your own) until you understand what has happened to the person's body and have had time to grasp what it means.

In this, the treatment center's rehabilitation team can help by giving you an evaluation of the person's limitations and potentialities.

Ideally, a rehabilitation team consists of all the professionals who have specific dealings with the patient during the time he or she undergoes treatment and training: that is, doctors, nurses, physical therapists, occupational therapists, psychologists, home-planning consultants, social workers, and vocational counselors.

From the physicians you will learn how the accident or illness affects the person's body and what medical treatment is necessary.

Nurses will familiarize you with procedures for proper patient care.

Through physical and occupational therapists you'll learn the techniques for active daily living being taught the patient, such as walking, reaching, grasping, transferring in and out of a wheelchair, getting dressed, preparing a meal.

Home-planning consultants recommend ways to modify a house or apartment so the patient can become as self-sufficient as possible.

Psychologists are available to help the patient adjust to what's happened to him, and meet informally with family members who wish to discuss their own concerns about the disabled.

Social workers and vocational counselors help guide you and the patient in ways to obtain from the community the assistance and services the patient may need for establishing an independent life.

This, according to those dedicated to the practice of rehabilitation medicine, is the way a team should function, the logic being that unless and until both patient and family are integrated into the treatment and recovery process, all the work done to rehabilitate the disabled will be for nothing. There'd be no point in training a patient to live independently if the family, or a responsible friend, don't know how to help the disabled one achieve it.

It is to the family's advantage, of course, to understand and support the rehabilitation process, because the sooner the disabled man or woman becomes self-sufficient, the sooner family members are free to go their own ways, too.

13

Not all rehabilitation centers are structured exactly the same way; some put more emphasis on one phase of treatment or training than on others. But in general, all of them recognize the need for an all-embracing patient-family approach and all have the same goal: making their patient as self-sufficient as possible.

As you might suspect, the facilities that can provide such comprehensive services are located in major metropolitan areas where large hospitals and medical schools can furnish talent and personnel, and where funds for research and practice can be generated.

Public and private hospitals in small cities, towns, and in rural areas usually can do little more than treat the disabling injury and shuttle the patient home as soon as possible; they haven't a staff diversified enough to supply all the techniques of rehabilitation medicine. In one sense, this is indicative of the hit-or-miss quality of medical care in this country today. Yet the medical community cannot be held responsible for the lack of a network of services for the disabled. For two hundred years the physically impaired were relegated to an unseen corner of society. Not until America was 201 years old did the barriers around the disabled begin to crack . . . when the disabled themselves mounted the attack.

What's more, the comprehensive approach to the practice of rehabilitation medicine, that of not only treating physical injury but tending the total person as well—including his or her psychological and social needs— is relatively new. It is a procedure conceived and implemented by Dr. Howard A. Rusk, founder and director of the Institute of Rehabilitation Medicine (IRM), New York University Medical Center, in New York City. Dr. Rusk points out in his autobiography, *A World to Care For*, that just a little over twenty-five years ago, in 1952, New York City was the only place in the nation that offered comprehensive rehabilitation to the disabled in its municipal hospitals, and that only sixty-five general hospitals across the country could, at that time, offer organized rehabilitation programs to their citizenry.

Still later, in 1972, Dr. Rusk estimated that despite the improvement in the kind and number of rehabilitation services available, "at least ten million disabled Americans still need rehabilitation and are not getting it. We'll have no reason to congratulate ourselves until the day when we assume that every disabled person has the right to rehabilitation, just as we now assume that everyone with a broken arm must have it set and splinted."[*]

So you do have the right to know all you can about your friend's or relative's problem, progress, and potential. You have the further right to be given specific information for getting comprehensive rehabilitation medical services if your local hospital cannot provide them.

Even in the smallest community, doctors, hard-pressed and overworked though they may be, do have access to directories, journals, and associations, as well as friends and colleagues in the medical profession from whom they can obtain information for you.

You cannot expect the doctors or nurses to make calls and write letters for you, but they can give you names, phone numbers, and addresses of rehabilitation centers and experts which you can use to arrange either for full-course treatment or for any portion of it that you and the rehab team feel would be most beneficial.

At various times during treatment, doctors and other members of the rehab team will begin to give you some idea about the extent of recovery their patient is likely to reach. However, no one experienced in rehabilitation medicine will say the disabled can't ever/won't ever accomplish something—walk, run, work, live alone, become president.

Over and over they witness the unbelievable happening: the boy born without arms or legs

---

[*] Howard A. Rusk, M.D., *A World to Care For* (New York: Random House, 1972), p. 289.

who, now fitted with artificial limbs, drives a jeep every day as manager of his uncle's cattle ranch; the teen-ager, now shopping for her first car, who as a newborn was considered to have little chance to survive.

Doctors and therapists could recite hundreds more such examples, proud of the techniques and innovations they've implemented to secure their patients' recovery, yet knowing that no surgical or medical procedure could pull off the miracles they've seen accomplished by the grit, courage, and determination of the disabled and their families.

The message to you is clear. Don't be too quick to accept the person's limitations as they appear to be. Be prepared to support the child's or adult's attempts to test himself even if it might mean a fall or two.

On the other hand, be ready to acknowledge that there are going to be certain limits within which the person will always have to operate. Once these are accepted by everyone, you and the disabled can arrange your lives accordingly.

In order to come to grips with the positive and the negative aspects of the limitations, it might help if you were to make a list of the things the person can do for himself or herself and a list of those things he or she cannot. With a clearer idea about the can-dos, you can leave the disabled free to make his or her own way, while you tend only to those things you and others will have to do: Christmas shopping, transportation, housekeeping or heavy cleaning, and the like.

Make a check list for task assignments so that the work load is shared by all members of the family and doesn't fall to just one. This will help avoid duplication of effort, as well as allow each person a legitimate amount of time out for rest and recreation. That is one of your rights, too.

Chapter 3

Ramps —Paths to Freedom

These gentle slopes are to the disabled as wings to a bird. Without them all wheels are square, every curb a prison.

In order for people with limited mobility to enter and leave their homes in wheelchairs they must either be carried, use mechanical lifts and hoists, or travel over ramps.

The first arrangement demands more than human strength and spirit can deliver except in emergencies. Power-driven aids are costly and limited in their application. By far the least expensive, most practical bridges to independence are ramps.

They are simple in design and, being triangular, are one of nature's most dependable forms. Although their shape is too basic to involve complicated building techniques, it's well-nigh impossible to make one correctly unless you understand slope requirements. Technically, slope involves degree of pitch and angle of gradient. Which means in ordinary English that

you shouldn't make the ramp too steep for the person who will use it.

The slope chart on page 20 will guide you in building or contracting for suitable ramps. In the last column of the chart are some terms that architects and engineers use in talking with each other about slope. Be aware of them in case you have dealings with building codes and zoning regulations.

From the chart you can see that ramps have one serious drawback: they need lots of space. The only way to make them shorter is to make them steeper. If you have space limitations at home, tell the rehabilitation team what they are. Better yet, take a drawing of the property to the evaluation meetings. The team can better advise you where ramps should be placed and recommend the aids and devices their patient will need for independent living at home.

Ramps are vital links between different levels, but don't think every doorstep has to have one.

16

Although it may be longer, one smooth connection between starting point and goal is less tiring to travel than a shorter route having many level changes and steep slopes.

Let the contour of the whole property, house and lot, help determine where a ramp should be. If a rear door is closer to ground level than the front, a ramp from the back may be more sensible. A side patio or porch might offer possibilities. If there's an attached garage, a ramp inside it may be all that's needed to get inside the house, via driveway, from some distant sidewalk.

Of course, the entrance you choose to ramp must be accessible from inside the house, too. No matter how precisely built, a ramp is only as good as all its approaches. Double-check width of doorways and hallways leading to the ramp inside the house; use the access measurements listed in Chapter 1 as a guide.

3–1 Framework for a basic ramp consists of treated lumber set on edge, braced, and end-nailed. For a gentle slope over a 6 in./152 mm step, ramp must extend 6 ft./1.8 m from platform edge.

Materials to Use

Ramps can be made of wood or masonry. Concrete is more expensive than wood in most instances, but lasts longer and is easier to maintain. Unless you're experienced in handling masonry, let professionals do the job while you supervise. Make sure they follow all your requirements for ramp slope and size.

If you plan to build ramps yourself, use wood. It's easy to handle, relatively inexpensive, and adapts to all weather conditions. Choose pressure-treated or naturally decay-resistant lumber. Figures 3–1 to 3–4 show how to construct a basic wooden ramp.

Another advantage of wood is that it lets you correct mistakes you're bound to make—not because you are inept but because the demands for slope, safety, and access are so rigid that only an engineering genius could succeed the first time around. So no matter what ramp material you use, get to know the more intimate details of ramp anatomy before hiring contractors or ordering supplies.

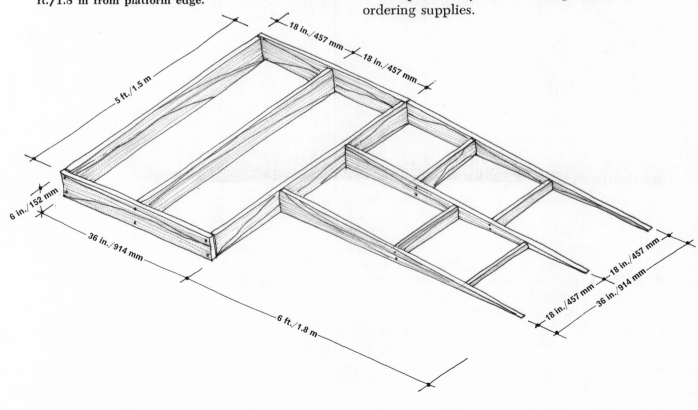

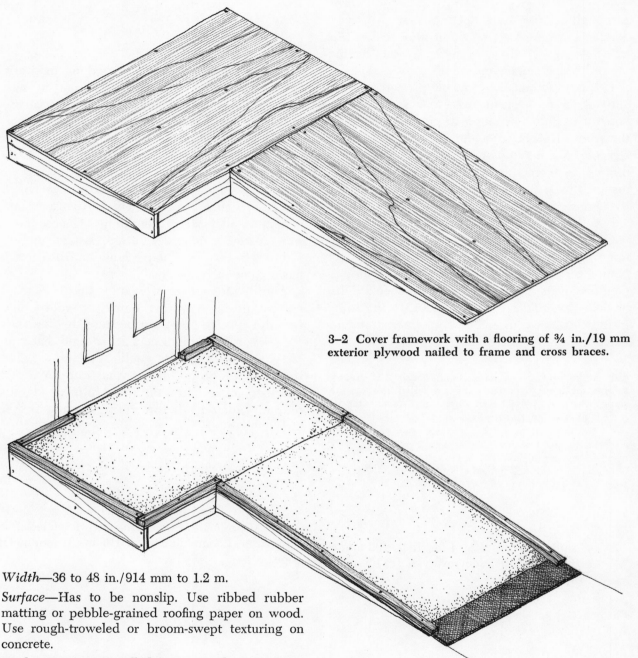

3–2 Cover framework with a flooring of ¾ in./19 mm exterior plywood nailed to frame and cross braces.

Width—36 to 48 in./914 mm to 1.2 m.

Surface—Has to be nonslip. Use ribbed rubber matting or pebble-grained roofing paper on wood. Use rough-troweled or broom-swept texturing on concrete.

Curbs—Sometimes called bumpers, these are continuous 2 × 4 in./51 × 102 mm strips laid flat on the surface of the ramp along both edges to act as wheel guides and provide knuckle space between wheels, or crutches, and the railings.

Flooring—Can be ¾ in./19 mm exterior plywood sheet, or 1 in./25 mm tongue-and-groove pine, or

3–3 Add curb (or bumper) strips along edges of ramp. Install nonslip surface (rough-textured roofing paper) with waterproof cement. *Note:* **A transition strip of ⅛ in./3 mm metal at end of ramp can be used to make a smoother connection between ramp and ground. Install it before you put on curbs or nonslip coating.**

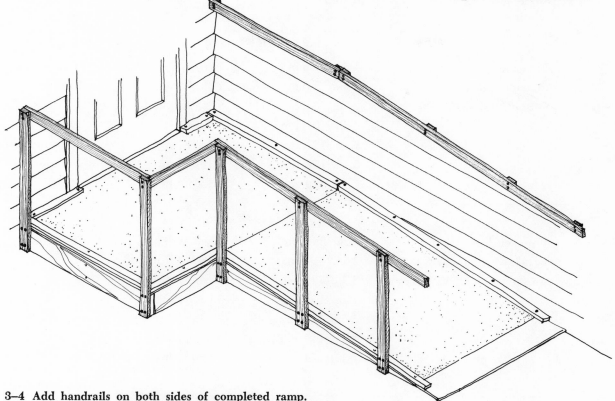

3–4 Add handrails on both sides of completed ramp. Space uprights 36 in./914 mm apart and fasten to base of ramp with four 5 in./127 mm lag screws per upright. Cut top ends of uprights at angle to accommodate slope of handrail to pitch of ramp. Top rail can be screwed to sides of uprights as here, or nailed to top ends. *Note:* Handrails can extend as much as 1 ft./ 305 mm beyond end of ramp unless protruding ends tend to catch clothing or be dangerous.

2 × 4 in./51 × 102 mm slats laid crosswise and spaced ⅜ in./9.5 mm apart.

Vertical supports—Use 2 × 4 in./51 × 102 mm or 4 × 4 in./102 × 102 mm every 6 ft./1.8 m on cement footings.

Supporting framework—Can be either 2 × 4 in./ 51 × 102 mm pine, or 1 × 6 in./25 × 152 mm treated lumber.

Finish—This is a matter of preference, but exterior paint or stain are the two most popular finishes. Boat or deck enamel are used frequently, too. Choose whatever is easiest for you to apply and maintain.

Clearance—Have a clear, level space of at least 6 ft./1.8 m at the bottom of the ramp so a wheelchair user can make turns or transfers.

Handrails—Be fussy about these. They are essential to the comfort and safety of the person who'll use the ramp, so they should be smooth and firmly anchored at both sides of the ramp. For adults, handrails should be 32 in./813 mm above surface of the ramp. For children, they should be from 16 to 18 in./406 to 457 mm high. If the handrail is installed on a wall, allow 2 in./51 mm for knuckle space. Make handrails out of smoothly sanded 2 × 4 in./51 × 102 mm lumber or 1¼ in./31 mm metal pipe.

Ramps can also be made of concrete, but unless you are very experienced, have this done by a contractor who is familiar with building codes and conditions of climate. Curbs or bumpers still have to be included, and the surface must be textured. The handrails and uprights of the concrete ramp in Figure 3–5 are made of 1¼ in./31 mm metal pipe.

Build a double-back ramp (see Figure 3–6) if there's not enough room for a long, straight one. Double-backs must have at each turn a

SLOPE CHART FOR RAMPS

Suit ramp to the user	Slope requirements	If step is this high . . .	. . . ramp must be this long	Ramp slope often referred to as . . .
I				
Gentle slope for most wheelchair users	For each 1 in./25 mm in height, the ramp must extend 12 in./305 mm	1 in./25 mm	1 ft./305 mm	"One in twelve"
		2 in./51 mm	2 ft./610 mm	1 in 12
		3 in./76 mm	3 ft./914 mm	1:12
		4 in./102 mm	4 ft./1.2 m	1/12
		5 in./127 mm	5 ft./1.5 m	"Five degree"
		6 in./152 mm	6 ft./1.8 m	5 degree
		7 in./179 mm	7 ft./2.1 m	5°
II				
For wheelchair users with *strong* arms; for those who *must* be pushed by able-bodied; for motorized chairs	For each 1 in./25 mm in height, the ramp must extend 9 in./229 mm	1 in./25 mm	9 in./229 mm	"Six degree"
		2 in./51 mm	18 in./457 mm	6 degree
		3 in./76 mm	27 in./686 mm	6°
		4 in./102 mm	36 in./914 mm	
		5 in./127 mm	45 in./1.1 m	
		6 in./152 mm	54 in./1.4 m	
		7 in./179 mm	63 in./1.6 m	
III				
Only for wheelchair users who are un- usually strong; when disabled is lightweight and pusher is strong; for extra-powerful motorized chairs	For each 1 in./25 mm in height, the ramp must extend 7 in./179 mm	1 in./25 mm	7 in./179 mm	"Eight degree"
		2 in./51 mm	14 in./356 mm	8 degree
		3 in./76 mm	21 in./533 mm	8°
		4 in./102 mm	28 in./711 mm	
		5 in./127 mm	35 in./889 mm	
		6 in./152 mm	42 in./1.07 m	
		7 in./179 mm	49 in./1.21 m	
IV				
Steepest slope —*only* for suitable motorized vehicles or mechanical assists such as incline lifts and power hoists	For each 1 in./25 mm in height, the ramp must extend 5 in./127 mm	1 in./25 mm	5 in./127 mm	"Ten degree"
		2 in./51 mm	10 in./254 mm	10 degree
		3 in./76 mm	15 in./381 mm	10°
		4 in./102 mm	20 in./508 mm	
		5 in./127 mm	25 in./635 mm	
		6 in./152 mm	30 in./762 mm	
		7 in./179 mm	35 in./889 mm	

A step of ⅝ in./15.9 mm or less need not be ramped.

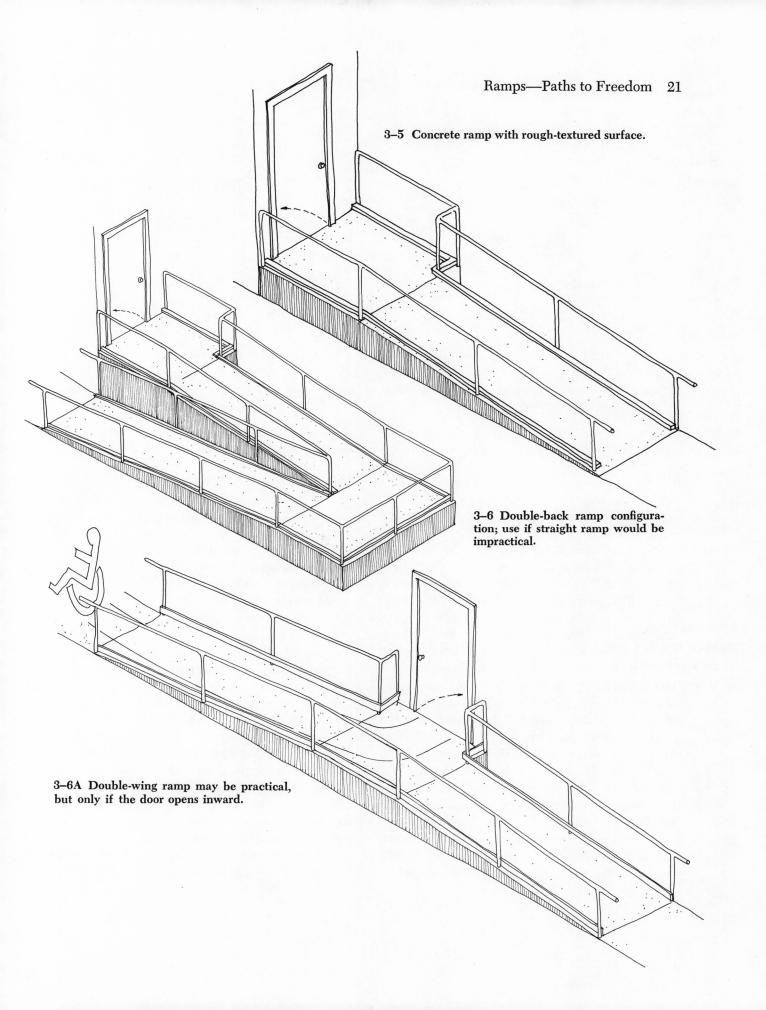

3–5 Concrete ramp with rough-textured surface.

3–6 Double-back ramp configuration; use if straight ramp would be impractical.

3–6A Double-wing ramp may be practical, but only if the door opens inward.

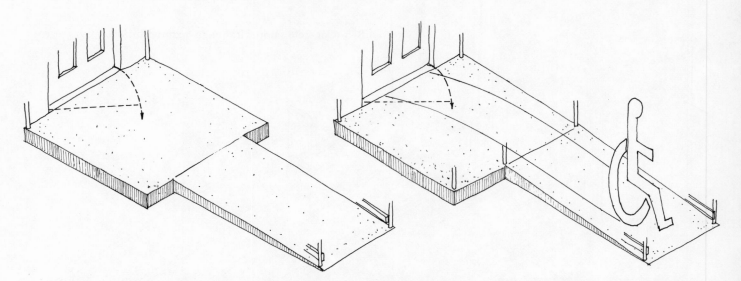

3–7 Ramps can extend from center of platform if door swings outward or swings inward.

3–8 If ramp must extend from side of platform, and if door swings *outward*, orient ramp to latch side of door.

level platform that's 5 ft./1.5 m deep so the wheelchair user can make a safe, comfortable turn. The base can be enclosed, left open, used for storage, softened with shrubs or vines.

The direction in which a door swings is all-important to proper platform size and ramp construction.

If a door swings outward, there should be a platform or level space beyond the door that's at least 5 ft./1.5 m deep and extends in width to 1 ft./305 mm beyond each side of the door-frame. An out-swinging door can have a ramp that extends from the center of the platform (as in Figure 3–7) or one that's situated toward the latch side of the door (as in Figure 3–8).

If the door swings inward, the platform need be only 3 ft./914 mm deep to provide adequate level space for opening the door from a seated position. (The platform still has to be wide enough to extend 1 ft./305 mm beyond each side of the doorframe.) However, situate the ramp at the hinge side of the door (see Figure 3–9); this allows a smooth arc of passage through the door to the ramp.

Just one of the many portable ramps you can buy is the metal one with the hinged handle shown in Figure 3–10. Available from Nelson

Medical Products, this model (No. 5037) sells for about $50 and is 36 in./914 mm long.

Other portable and large folding ramps for vans and cars can be obtained from Handi-Ramp, Inc. Powered lifts, hoists, and elevators for inside and outside the house come from such companies as American Stair Glide Corporation and the Cheney Company. They each have distribution centers across the country and can supply current brochures and addresses of dealers near you. They, and others, are listed in the Yellow Pages under Elevators.

Financial Help Available

While power-lift equipment is expensive, running from several hundred dollars up into the thousands, it can be classified as a medical expense for income tax purposes. Call your regional Internal Revenue Service office to find out exactly what the disabled must do to qualify.

Your state vocational rehabilitation office may also be able to help cover some or all of the costs for powered equipment if it can be established, to the agency's satisfaction, that the lift is essential for getting the disabled person out

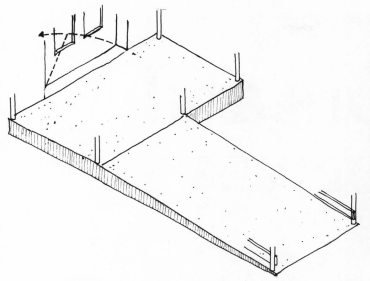

Mainstream Source List—Ramps and Lifts

American Stair Glide Corp.
4001 East 138th Street
Glenview, Missouri 64030

Handi-Ramp, Inc.
1414 Armour Boulevard
Mundelein, Illinois 60060

Nelson Medical Products
5690 Sarah Avenue
Sarasota, Florida 33581

The Cheney Company
7611 North 73rd Street
Milwaukee, Wisconsin 53223

3–9 If ramp must extend from side of platform, and if door swings *inward*, orient ramp to hinge side of door.

of the house in order to go to work, go to school, or take care of home and family. Look in the telephone book for the local vocational rehabilitation listing.

3–10 A portable metal ramp you can buy, made by Nelson Medical.

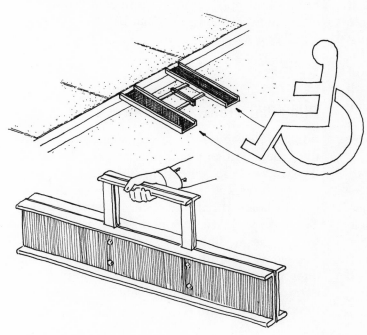

Chapter 4

Doors and Doorways

Reach. Grasp. Twist. Pull. Back up. Turn. Go around. Repeat all over again. That's getting a door open and closed. No wonder the physically disabled declare doors are energy-sapping, frustrating barriers they'd gladly do without. Some are necessary for privacy and safety, such as entry doors and those at bathroom and bedroom. Basement stairways and other dangerous openings in a home should be blocked also. But in general, regard every door as an expendable barrier that you should either remove or at least make easier to operate.

Side-hinged swing-out doors are the most difficult for the disabled to handle. Almost all doors inside the house will be of this kind. Either prop them open permanently or take them off their hinges and store them—under beds and behind a sofa if need be.

Heavy two-way swinging doors, usually on kitchens in older homes and apartments, are of no benefit to anyone with limited mobility. Mark these for extinction. French and other two-leaf doors which require opening first one and then the other in order to get through are worse than useless. They should be kept open, removed altogether, or replaced with folding or sliding doors.

Any door that sticks, binds, or drags is a double barrier. Simply removing old paint and oiling the hinges may correct the problem. More stubborn cases might call for taking the door down, planing and sanding the edges, and rehanging on new hardware.

If it seems that only a new door will do, consider the preassembled replacement kind sold in building supply stores. These come complete with frame, prehung door, and instructions for installation.

Sills and Thresholds

Inside the house, these should be removed—all of them. Put an identifying mark with crayon on each one and store them in case they have to be put back at some future time.

Thresholds at entry doors are another matter; they help keep weather and drafts out, so they have to be modified rather than removed.

A wooden threshold can be beveled on both sides to form a sort of miniature ramp, as in Figure 4–1. Add weather stripping to the door to seal out drafts.

24

Ready-made thresholds, such as the metal one by Macklanburg-Duncan shown being installed in Figure 4–2, are beveled on both sides and have a vinyl strip in the center to help seal out the weather. Hardware stores and building supply centers carry them.

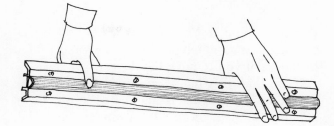

4–2 Buy ready-made thresholds, install them yourself.

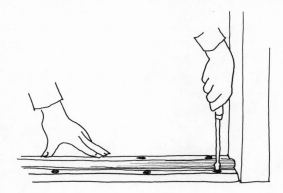

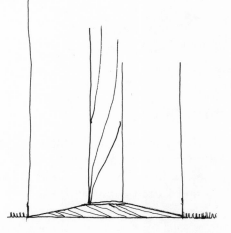

4–1 Wooden thresholds can be beveled with plane, file, or saw.

If You Rent

Some landlords are understanding and will let you remove doors and doorsills provided you agree to put them back when you or the tenant moves out. Others won't be happy about the idea at all. But if the house or apartment is just what you want, don't press the subject further. Move in and remove the doors later. Store hardware, sill, and door together; otherwise you'll have the dickens of a time putting them back in their original location.

Dimensions Are Critical

Measure the width of doorways very carefully because, to someone in a wheelchair, fractions of an inch (millimeters) can either permit access or totally block it.

Notice the emphasis is on doorway rather than door. A door is simply a covering which, if it's a hindrance for one reason or another, can be taken away or replaced with something more suitable. There's nothing flexible about a doorway, however. It is rooted in its own dimensions and, if too narrow, is as impenetrable as a brick wall.

Doorways that are 32 in./813 mm wide will accommodate people in wheelchairs as well as those using crutches, canes, and the like. Some doorways are 36 in./914 mm wide; these are ideal.

The most comfortable level for doorknobs is 36 in./914 mm above the floor.

Kickplates will protect doors from the scrapes and gouges caused by wheelchairs, crutches, and braces. Use either metal or plastic ones.

Widening Doorways

When a doorway is fitted with a side-hinged door as most are, its clear opening is made narrower by the thickness of the door itself as it stands wide open. You automatically widen the opening, by as much as 2 in./51 mm in some instances, if you remove the door.

If, on the other hand, you need the door and the 2 in./51 mm gain is adequate, consider rehanging the door on fold-back hinges. Then the door will no longer protrude into the doorway but will fold flat against the wall. Fold-back hinges fit the same three holes drilled for ordinary hinges, so landlords shouldn't object to the swap. Those in Figure 4–3 are from MED, Inc., and cost about $15 a pair.

The doorframe itself can yield valuable extra space if you carefully pry off the doorjamb strips on one or both sides.

A last resort is to widen the doorway structurally by stripping off the entire frame and

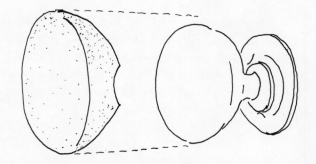

4–4 Foam knob cover makes round doorknobs easier to grip.

•

Off with Knobs

Since nothing about today's doors is right as far as the disabled are concerned, you won't be too surprised to learn that doorknobs should be packed up and stored along with sills and rusty hinges.

Anyone who is seated, uses crutches, has poor coordination, or has a weak grip has difficulty twisting round, smooth doorknobs. You can remedy the situation by making the knobs bigger.

A thick foam cover can be slipped over the knob. Some, such as the one in Figure 4–4, are sold in notions departments as protectors to keep the knob from marring an adjacent wall. You can also fashion a knob collar of thick double-faced foam tape covered by wide strips of old suede or chamois.

Better yet, replace knobs with lever-type handles. These are ideal for the physically disabled because pressure with forearm, wrist, or elbow will unlatch the door.

Unfortunately, though, handles of this kind are not readily available to the average homeowner. Most are designed and made for commercial and institutional use. Few hardware stores carry them, and those that do have a limited selection. The majority are imported from Europe and, though beautifully designed, are both expensive and available in this country only through architects, contractors, and deco-

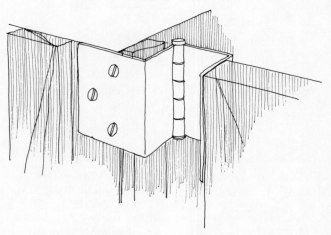

4–3 Fold-back hinges can replace conventional door hinges.

cutting a larger opening. This means ripping through existing studs, adding a new header and supports, and sheathing the raw cut to match surrounding surfaces. It's a job experienced Sunday carpenters might handle, but it is not one for outright amateurs. Also, if a door has to be hung in the new opening, get help, because hanging doors properly is a tricky business.

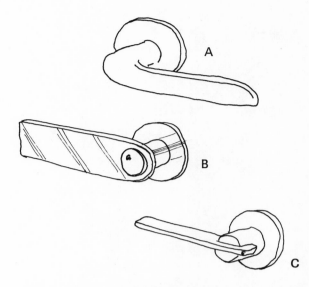

4–5 Open-end door handles, easier to operate than round knobs.

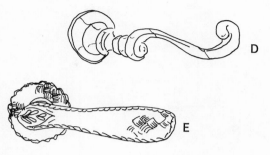

4–6 Door handles can be decorative as well as functional.

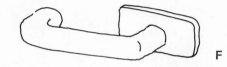

4–7 Closed-end door lever, ideal for the disabled.

rators. But since levers are such a convenience for the disabled, it's worthwhile making the effort to find them.

Levers A, B, and C in Figure 4–5 are typical of the open-end designs made of polished and brushed chrome or brass. Larger hardware stores stock them. Levers D and E in Figure 4–6 are representative of the luxurious styles and finishes available from specialized and decorative hardware stores.

A closed-end lever (sometimes called a safety lever) is ideal for the disabled since the curved end is not apt to catch on sleeves and pockets. Thick, tubular, and smooth, it feels gentle to sensitive hands. An example is F in Figure 4–7. Made of solid nylon in nine vivid colors, this British import can be ordered by the contractor or decorator from The Ironmonger.

Automatic Doors

Perhaps in the next decade our homes and apartments will have doors that glide silently in and out of walls at some secret signal. Now all we can do is experience their magic at airports and supermarkets and see them in science fiction movies. But it is obvious that automatic doors do exist even for houses because the technology for them is already here. It is a matter of time and money; one standard-sized fully automatic sliding door, today, costs nearly $3,000. Let's hope that building techniques soon will be such that electronic doors will be as much a part of standard residential equipment as gas or electric ranges.

Until that happy day, you can consider the remote-controlled door-opening devices that are obtainable. One, the Silent Swing electromechanical operator from Stanley Door Operating Equipment, a division of the Stanley Works, is no bigger than a bread box and can be mounted on the wall directly above the door. Pictured in Figure 4–8, this opener is for lightweight interior doors and can be activated by radio transmitter or push-button switch. It uses 110-volt household current and, depending upon the kind of control mechanism you choose (switch or radio), costs from $600 to $730.

If anyone needs an automatic garage-door opener, the disabled homeowner does. Happily, such equipment is easy to find these days and is

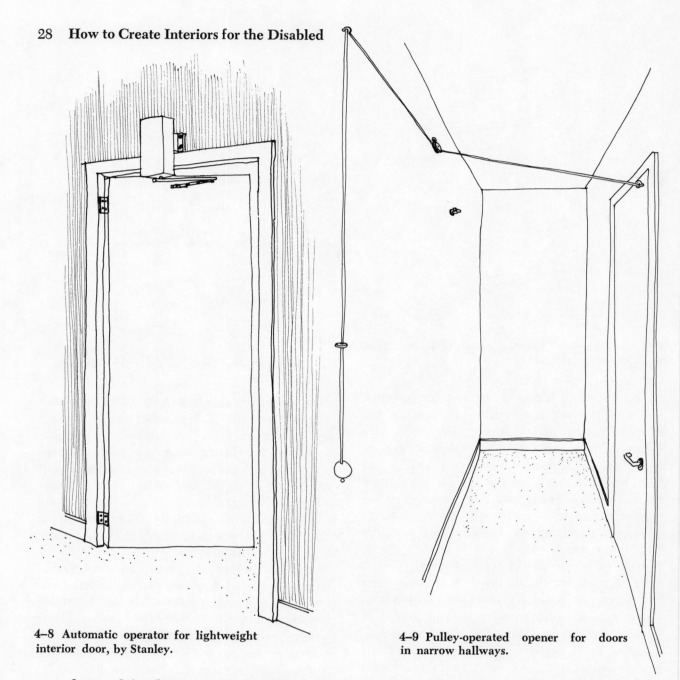

4–8 Automatic operator for lightweight interior door, by Stanley.

4–9 Pulley-operated opener for doors in narrow hallways.

even designed for do-it-yourself installation. JC Penney, for one, can supply a radio-controlled system, complete, for approximately $160.

Rig Your Own Door Opener

With a length of venetian-blind cord (it's treated to be abrasion-resistant), one forty-cent pulley, and three or four screw eyes you can fashion an effective, though funny-looking, door opener for practically nothing (see Figure 4–12). This door, in an awkward corner, can be opened by someone sitting or standing at a distance from it.

Fasten one end of the venetian-blind cord to a screw eye at the top corner of the door. Run the cord through a pulley fixed to the ceiling at

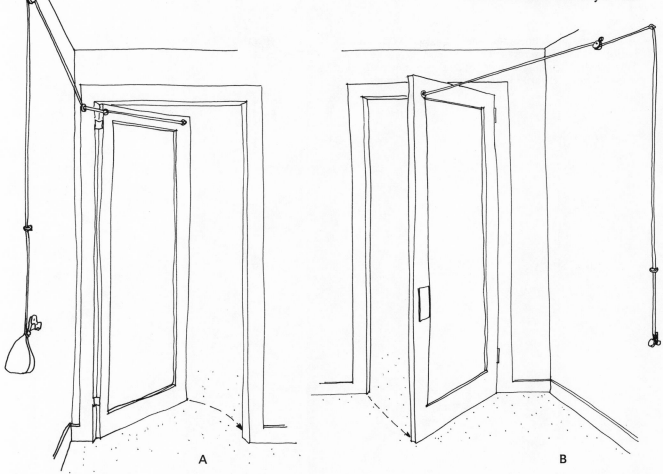

A B

4–10 Pulley-operated door closer (A); the counter-weight is a bag of sand. If door is counterweighted, pulley cord on opposite side must be anchored (B).

a point that's about 4 ft./1.2 m from the door-frame and 8 in./203 mm from the side wall. Draw the cord outward from the pulley at a slight angle toward the wall. Feed the cord down through a line of screw eyes on the wall. Push the cord through the center of a medium-sized rubber ball, knot it on the underside, and cut off the excess cord. A downward pull on the ball will cause the door to open.

This ball-and-cord door opener can be rigged in a hallway in the same manner (see Figure 4–9), only here the pulley is mounted on the opposite wall at a point that's slightly higher than the top edge of the door. (This prevents the

door from getting tangled in the cord.) A small vinyl-tipped doorstop should be set high enough on the wall to be out of the way, yet keep the door from swinging back too far.

A door will swing closed if it has a counter-weight on the opposite side (see Figure 4–10,A). Run the cord through two screw eyes attached to the top of the door at the corners. Run the cord through another screw eye on the edge of the doorframe. Thread the cord through a pulley that's been fixed to the side wall at a point slightly higher than the top edge of the door-frame (to aid leverage). Drop the cord straight down from the pulley through two or three screw eyes. Knot the cord around a heavy cloth bag filled with enough sand (or old doorknobs) to pull the door closed, gently.

To hold a counterweighted door open yet

4–11 Parts of homemade door opener: (A) metal pulley, (B) metal screw eye, (C) metal or plastic knob, (D) plastic right-angle doorstop, (E) rubber ball, (F) wooden ring or yarn-wrapped embroidery hoop.

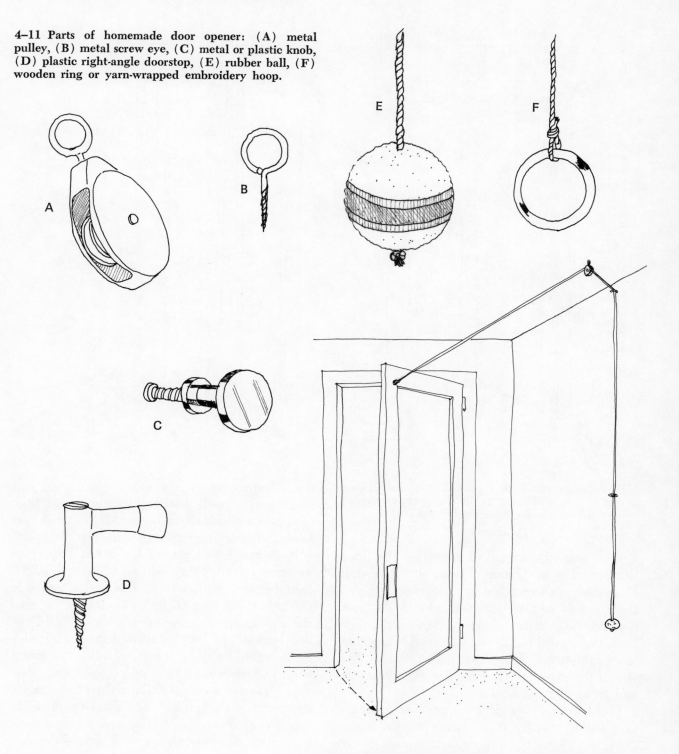

4–12 Homemade pulley-operated opener for in-swinging door in awkward corner.

make it convenient to close when desired, fashion a loop in the cord part way up from the end. Fit this loop over a small knob set at a handy spot on the wall (see Figure 4–10,B). When the loop is released, the door will close. Allow enough length below the loop so the cord can be retrieved easily.

In addition to venetian-blind cord, what you'll need to make up your own door openers are these bits and pieces (see Figure 4–11):

A. Small metal pulley, 2½ in./64 mm
B. Metal screw eyes, 1¼ in./31 mm
C. Small metal or plastic knob
D. Plastic right-angle doorstop
E. Rubber ball, large or medium
F. Large, smooth wooden ring or yarn-wrapped embroidery hoop

Of course, using manual door openers takes a certain amount of physical strength. Be aware of what the disabled child or adult can do be-fore you install any mechanical aid, homemade or automatic. Maybe one of these days something better will come along. Until it does, the only thing to do is—make do.

Mainstream Source List—Doors and Doorways

The Ironmonger
446 N. Wells Street
Chicago, Illinois 60610

Macklanburg-Duncan Co.
P.O. Box 25188
Oklahoma City, Oklahoma 73125

MED, Inc.
1215 South Harlem Avenue
Forest Park, Illinois 60130

Stanley Door Operating Equipment Automatic Silent Swing interior door opener distributed by:

Fred G. MacKenzie Co., Inc.
107 Reade Street
New York, N.Y. 10013

Chapter 5

Windows

"Which shall it be," asked the magician, "one room with a window or a palace with none?"

"One room, if you please," said the poet.

"For the solitude?" asked the magician.

"For the life of me," answered the poet.

Do all you can to make windows accessible and easy to operate, for they are important links between the disabled person and his or her total environment. Not being able to see out can provoke feelings of despair and alienation in all of us, especially in those whose mobility is limited.

When you are ready to buy new windows, either as replacements for old ones or for new construction, choose sliding, awning, or casement windows. These are easy to handle since they can be pushed or pulled open and closed with one hand, wrist, or forearm while seated or standing.

A Comfortable Height

Window sills should be between 30 and 36 in./762 mm and 914 mm above the floor. Look for these critical dimensions as you shop for a house or apartment; specify them in plans for a new home or room addition.

•

Windows to Have and Why

If an existing house or apartment has cranky old windows throughout, don't think all of them have to be junked; replace a few at a time. It's easier on the budget, and you, to concentrate on the ones used frequently, and add others gradually as time and money allow. Besides, if you're renting, two, maybe three window replacements are about all you can expect a landlord to permit.

Since awning, casement, and sliding windows each require different combinations of strength and movement to operate, be aware of what the child or adult can handle and choose accordingly.

Horizontal sliding windows glide open on tracks at top and bottom. While their tablike handles are usually small and placed too high to reach while seated, the sashes are made to glide smoothly and will move quite well when pulled or pushed at the bottom. To make opening and closing easier, you could fasten one or two more handles (tab-shaped or D-shaped) lower down on the operating sash. Pad the handles with strips of foam, sponge, or cloth held in place with glue.

5–1 Horizontal sliding windows.

Awning windows are top pivoted and can be pushed outward from the bottom. Some, like the one in Figure 5–2, are combined with a fixed pane of glass above or below. Most companies make this kind, but they also have individual awning windows that you can arrange in stacks or rows, or use singly. Awnings are generally the easiest windows for the disabled to handle; they are low enough to be reached, and can be pushed or pulled from a straight-on position. However, their latches are designed not to interfere with draperies and curtains, so are small and difficult to grip. You could add a metal bar across the bottom for easier pushing, and a length of cord fastened in the center of the bottom rail for pulling. If you decide upon awning windows, have only a few. They are small, don't open wide, and are a safety hazard in case of fire.

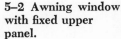

5–2 Awning window with fixed upper panel.

Casement windows swing open on hinges mounted at the side. In Europe, most casements open inward, but in this country they swing outward and for this reason should not be used near walkways or where people can bump into the open sash. As a rule, casements are operated by crank handles that are small, hard to grip, and sometimes out of reach. You might consider installing an over-the-sill crank (some manufacturers have them), or enlarging the handle with cloth, yarn wrapping, or perhaps a sponge-rubber ball.

If you're handy, you can install awning, casement, or sliding windows yourself. Andersen,

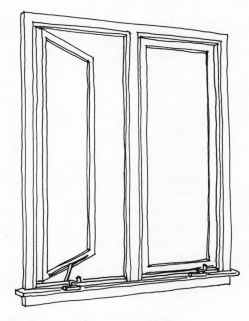

5–3 Casement windows, out-swinging.

for one, stocks all three as fully assembled replacement units ready to fit into existing or newly shaped openings. To get an idea of what's involved, write the company for a free copy of their illustrated, step-by-step instruction booklet. Also, ask about their Perma-Shield casement, gliding, or awning windows: not only are these weather-tight and maintenance-free (due to a tough vinyl sheath bonded to the frame), but they are designed to operate with minimum effort. Furthermore, this company's pretreated wooden-framed awning windows, usually fitted with rotor operators, can be had with simple awning locks instead. (These are similar to the ordinary quarter-turn cam locks you find on double-hung windows, except here they are set vertically rather than horizontally.) Pushing on the lock with the heel of the hand releases the latch, and the window can then be pushed open manually.

Another maker of easy-to-handle windows is Pella. Their awning and casement windows are specially designed to open smoothly, as well as glide to a center pivot (in an open position) so both surfaces of the window can be cleaned from inside the house. Even their double-hung windows tilt inward on center pivots in order to make window washing less of a chore. For a free illustrated booklet, write Pella Rolscreen Company.

See What You're Getting

It pays to visit dealer showrooms and have them give you a demonstration before you decide upon what windows to buy. Look in the Yellow Pages under Windows for the dealers nearest you and ask to be shown full-sized windows. Scaled-down miniature models are no help at all in determining how well suited to a particular disability a window will be.

That Other Window

Double-hung windows are awful. Even the able-bodied have trouble getting them up, down, washed, and dried. How a design this awkward became so widely accepted defies imagination. But it did and we're stuck with double-hung windows in more ways than one; they are standard fixtures in the majority of today's buildings and, unfortunately, show no sign of being declared inane.

If you own your home or have a landlord who is part saint, you can of course install something more sensible. But if you rent or just need more time to judge how the spirit of independence is holding up in your disabled friend or relative, try one of these home remedies. Although they are not professional and won't be suitable everywhere, the ideas might spark some of your own.

If big, bulky air conditioners can be set into a double-hung window opening, why not an awning window (see Figure 5–4) that you make yourself? *Note*: The window must open inward, for safety and legal reasons, but it can be hinged at top or bottom. Use tempered glass; it's more expensive than ordinary glass but safer. Raise the window to the height you want the new window to be, then measure the opening. You'll need four frames in all, each to fit inside the other (see Figure 5–5):

A. A wood-framed glass panel (the sash).
B. A frame for the sash: make it deep enough to hold the flush-mounted sash and also serve as a ledge on which the old sash will rest.
C. A jamb for the awning to close against: use molding strips fastened all around the inside of the sash frame.
D. An anchoring flange: wood strips to fit like a collar around the sash frame and form the structure through which you fit screws to fasten the whole assembly to the face of the existing window frame.

For hardware, you will need a continuous hinge and one storm sash adjuster set, composed of one pull handle and two friction hinge arms that hold the window open at any position. These are sold in hardware stores.

Another suggestion, putting doors in windows, is inspired by plastics that are suitable for glazing, such as Lexan and Plexiglas. (In the Yellow Pages look for authorized dealers under Plastics as well as Windows.)

For example, consider removing the glass from the bottom sash of an old double-hung window and fitting the top half of the opening with one

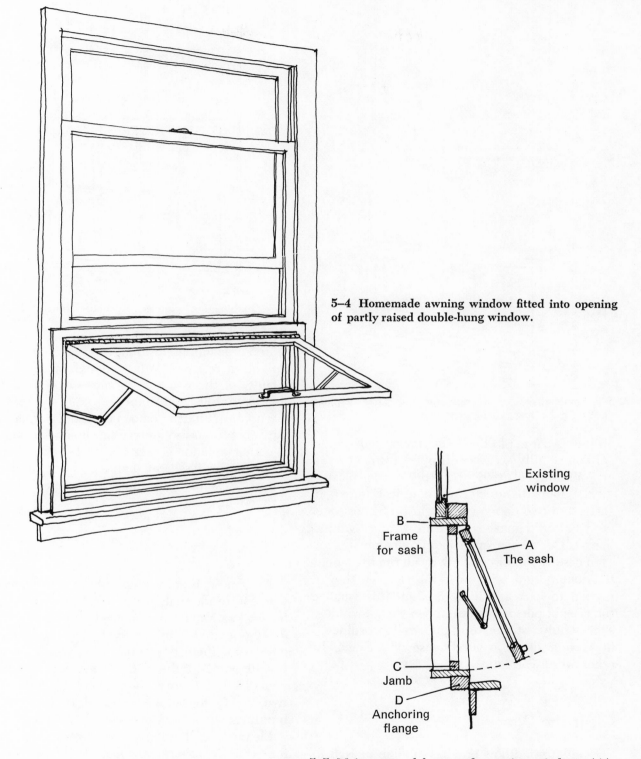

5–4 Homemade awning window fitted into opening of partly raised double-hung window.

Existing window

B
Frame for sash

A
The sash

C
Jamb

D
Anchoring flange

5–5 Main parts of homemade awning window: (A) sash, (B) frame for sash, (C) jamb, (D) anchoring flange.

5–6 Small easy-to-open doors for a window; replace glass with the new glazing plastics.

5–7 Double-hung window, especially difficult for the disabled to use.

of the glazing plastics. The lower half could contain a fully weather-stripped frame (wood or aluminum) fitted with two little plastic-glazed doors that open inward, as in Figure 5–6. Instead of two doors, you might prefer just one. Or you could make an inward-tilting awning-like sash, or even a small sliding window.

In case anyone wonders why all the fuss about the double-hung window in this chapter, they're invited to look at Figure 5–7 and to visualize the type of person who can open such a window successfully: strong, upright, well coordinated in all four limbs, a good sense of balance. In other words, athletic.

Clear the Way

Keep in mind how one has to align oneself in order to operate a window: head on from a seated or standing position; from an angle; close up and at one side. Allow enough space in the vicinity of the window for the person to travel to and from it comfortably.

There isn't much you can do about permanent barriers such as radiators except to enclose them. Wooden radiator covers are preferred because they transfer less heat than metal ones and are not as likely to cause injury if bumped into or scraped against.

No Magic, Yet

As of now, there are no automated windows. Current residential fire and safety regulations forbid (with good reason) our having electronically operated windows even though the technology for them does exist. Somewhere, in the private homes of the world's electronic geniuses, you can bet there's an automatic window or two, ready to be incorporated in tomorrow's buildings when the time is ripe.

Meanwhile, there are remote-control systems for window coverings. One, from the Kirsch Company, allows you to open and close draperies

5–8 For vertical louvered blinds, allow at least 2 ft./ 610 mm of open space at approach side of pull cord.

5–9 Decorated window shade enlivens a child's room.
Pulley latch (inset), fastened to sill, controls pull cord.

from anywhere in a room by pushing a button on a portable console. Another, by Alcan Aluminum Corporation, operates louvered window blinds. One or several blinds can be opened and closed —from bed, desk, or hallway—by push button.

Keep It Simple

The disabled appreciate attractively dressed windows as much as anyone, but they like simplicity more. A complicated arrangement of drapery over sheer curtains over blinds is too much to take care of. Totally bare windows, on the other hand, are stark and forbidding unless softened by hanging plants (which constitute another problem). It's better to have either tailored tiebacks, roll-up window shades with long cords, lightweight draw draperies with easy-to-get-at pull-cord, or louvered blinds.

Vertical louvered blinds are a simple one-layer covering that imparts the feeling of draperies yet controls light and air. Verticals such as those in Figure 5–8 are simple to operate provided the pull-cord bracket is wall-mounted at a comfortable height, and there's ample clear space in the vicinity to accommodate a person who is seated or standing.

An attractive window treatment is shown in Figure 5–9. At one window of this child's room designed by Michael Kennedy for JC Penney is a light-hearted shade with a painted-on apple tree. Extra-long cord, passed through a small pulley latch fastened to the sill, helps raise and lower the shade with little effort. (Since another window in this room is used all the time and this one is not, the wooden table and plant cause no accessibility problems.) This room is part of the new wing built by Mary and Bill Walker for their daughter, Betsy. A family friend painted the design on the window shade. We will have more to say about Betsy's room in Chapter 11.

Mainstream Source List—Windows

Alcan Aluminum Corporation
Warren, Ohio 44482

Andersen Corporation
Bayport, Minnesota 55003

The Kirsch Company
309 North Prospect
Sturgis, Michigan 49091

Pella Rolscreen Company
Pella, Iowa 50219

Chapter 6

Power, Light, Communications

Each year the miracle of electronics technology produces hundreds of gadgets and ultra-sophisticated equipment to help, amuse, and sometimes confound us. No group of people waits for each new discovery more eagerly than the disabled, for there is clear evidence that the wondrous forces and frequencies plucked from our cosmic supermarket to compute mathematical formulas and drive machinery might soon furnish something their own physical circuitry cannot: surrogate sources of power.

Already, scientists are searching for ways to couple electronics with whatever strengths the body has—eye blinks, respiration—to operate household appliances, guide wheelchairs, communicate over distances.

Even now, radio waves open doors, cook food, move toys to and fro. It also appears that invisible light rays and inaudible sound waves will create a new generation of useful products and services for the marketplaces of the future. Right now, though, the disabled must go on building active daily lives for themselves with the goods that are available, in ways best suited to their special needs.

A Personal Control Center

In movies, magazines, and newspapers, you've seen fabulous headboards, chairs, and chests studded with dials and switches for operating by remote control everything from coffeepots to movie projectors. You've seen the four-figure price tags, too; but if you're willing to forgo padded upholstery and professional designer fees, you can put together an inexpensive control center for any room in the house.

At the heart of such a control center could be the little 9 × 3 × 3 in./229 × 76 × 76 mm electrical outlet strip console in Figure 6–1. It contains six "U" ground outlets, each controlled by its own switch and pilot light. (The plug-in outlets are at the rear.) It's available

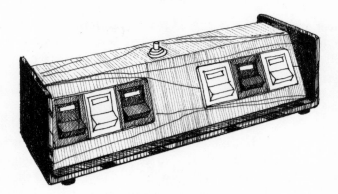

6–1 Small electrical tabletop strip console has six outlets, switches.

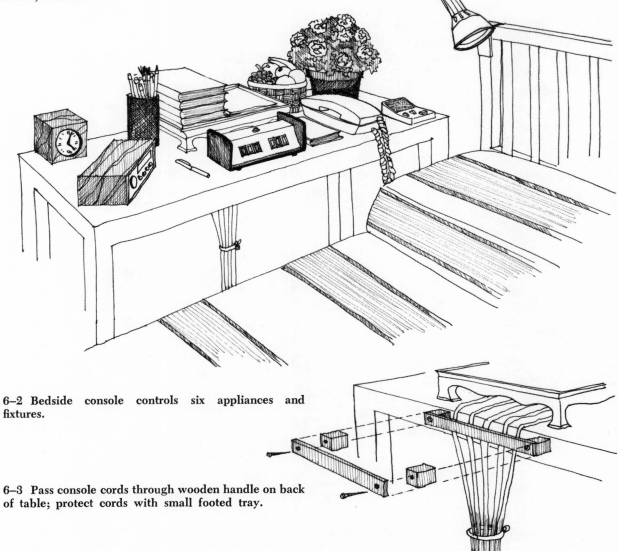

6–2 Bedside console controls six appliances and fixtures.

6–3 Pass console cords through wooden handle on back of table; protect cords with small footed tray.

with circuit breaker or fuse and either a 6 ft./ 1.2 m or a 15 ft./3.8 m heavy-duty cord set. Rated at 15 amperes, 130 volts, and made by SGL Waber Electric (Model No. 96), it can be ordered from Atlas Electronics Corporation in New York City for approximately $35 plus handling and shipping.

Plugged into the strip console, in Figure 6–2, are (for example) a bed lamp, a table lamp, an air conditioner, a television set, a stereo, and a small intercom set. (More about the intercom below.) All six appliances can be switched on or off from the bedside console. On the table in addition to the console (in the middle) are a battery-powered clock and radio, pencils, books, flowers, snack food, and a small footed tray.

Since six electric cords sprouting from the console could become a tangled mess, a wooden or rope handle (not a metal one) should be fixed to the table edge (see Figure 6–3) and all the cords passed through the handle. Tie the cords loosely together with a strip of fabric; again, do not use metal. To protect the cords further and

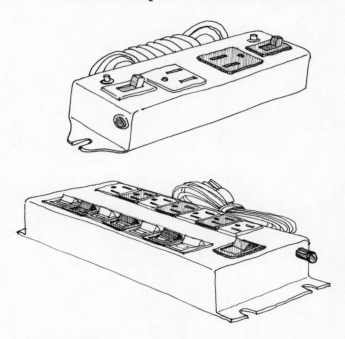

6–4 Electrical outlet strips are also available without console cover.

regain the table space they occupy, cover them with a small footed tray—wood or lacquer— glued in place or weighted down with books, magazines—whatever.

A Parsons table is used here because of its long, narrow shape and sturdy legs that can be fitted with ball casters. The legs could also be cut down or built up on blocks if it's necessary to adjust the table height. Parsons tables are available in many finishes and sizes, though the narrow ones, 16 and 18 in./406 and 457 mm wide, are best for the disabled. This one from JC Penney measures 18 × 48 in./457 mm × 1.2 m, comes ready to finish, and costs about $55.

To make it easier to push or pull the table into position (if you've added casters), fasten a D-shaped handle to one edge or attach a length of cord to the table and side of the bed.

Choose Extension Cords Wisely

In order to connect lamps and appliances to the control console, you will need quite a few extension cords. Be sure to use the right kind of extension cord for lamps, stereo, and intercom; heavy-duty three-prong cords for heaters, air conditioners, and the like. Also, since you will have so many cords to keep track of, tie them loosely together at intervals with fabric strips and lay them out along the floor around the edges of the room; do not have any crossing the center of the floor or lying under rugs or carpets.

Electrical outlet strips, unadorned by a console cover, are ideal for use by the disabled provided they have the safety and convenience features the one in Figure 6–4 has: a built-in pilot light on all switches; a master on-off switch and circuit breaker; a long heavy-duty cord. This seven-switch outlet by SGL Waber (Model No. 25P) is available for about $38 from Atlas Electronics Corporation.

Wall Switches and Outlets

Through pressures exerted by the disabled themselves, building standards are slowly being modified to make certain built-in conveniences more accessible to all people, disabled and non-disabled alike. One of these modifications calls for placing wall switches and outlets at more comfortable levels. For instance, light switches that are 36 in./914 mm above the floor are ideal

6–6 Wireless remote-control switch.

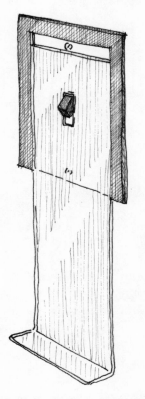

6–5 Light-switch extender slips over standard switch-plate.

for everyone, whether seated or standing. Outlets 18 in./457 mm above the floor are also more convenient, and many recent buildings have adopted these new placement levels. Nevertheless, millions of homes and apartments still are full of such fixtures that are difficult if not impossible to reach. As a result, there's a thriving market of all kinds of useful gadgets and devices

for connecting and operating lamps and appliances with less effort.

A light-switch extender that slips over a standard switchplate is available for about $4 from Maddak, Inc. (see Figure 6–5). The handle at the bottom of the sliding plastic strip makes it easy for a child or seated adult to operate the light switch. The strip is 22 in./559 mm long.

The wireless remote-control switch shown in Figure 6–6 turns on lamps, television, and the like via sound-command produced by a hand-held transmitter. However, it requires a squeezing action, so the person using it needs a firm grip and good hand coordination. It costs about $15, and can be ordered from Hammacher Schlemmer in New York City.

The squat table-top dimmer-lighter in Figure 6–7 can't tip over. Its wide disk-shaped switch can be operated with the palm of the hand.

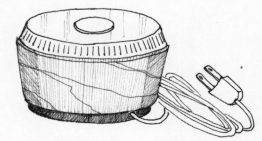

6–7 Tabletop dimmer-lighter switch.

Made by Lutron, it is available from Hammacher Schlemmer for approximately $20.

Operating old-fashioned push-button and toggle switches requires a certain amount of well-coordinated strength that some adults and children do not have. Fortunately, you can replace these switches with new silent ones that have wide rocker-arm handles (see Figure 6–8). A rocker-arm switch can be activated with a gentle tap or by sliding hand or wrist along its edge. Made to fit standard wall boxes, rocker switches can be had with either plain handles or lighted handles that glow in the dark, and are available at your nearest hardware or home-center store.

Thank goodness, all the new silent switches are made to fit standard wall boxes, so replacing the old with the new is relatively simple. What's more, they come in an array of styles, with features you'll find helpful for special situations. For example, three-way wall switches—two switches in different locations that control the same light—or pilot-light wall switches with handles that glow when a light is on in some place not readily seen, such as an attic, basement, or garage.

Completely silent timer switches are another recent arrival. Their function is to hold a light or appliance on for a preselected period of time: for thirty minutes, for an hour, even for twelve hours. One variety will hold a light on permanently but can also act as an interval timer when needed.

Dimmer switches are particularly handy for

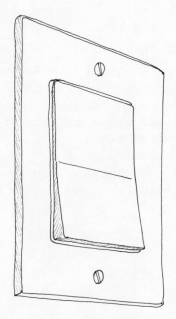

6–8 Rocker-arm switch is wide, easy to use.

6–9 Plug-in timer with big numerals.

the disabled, too. Not only can dimmers control intensity of light and thereby conserve electricity, but they are designed with thick, dial-like knobs that are easy to grip or rotate with the side of the hand or wrist. Choose dimmers with a push-on, push-off dial switch; some have knobs that must be gripped and turned on and off, and that's not always easy for some people to do.

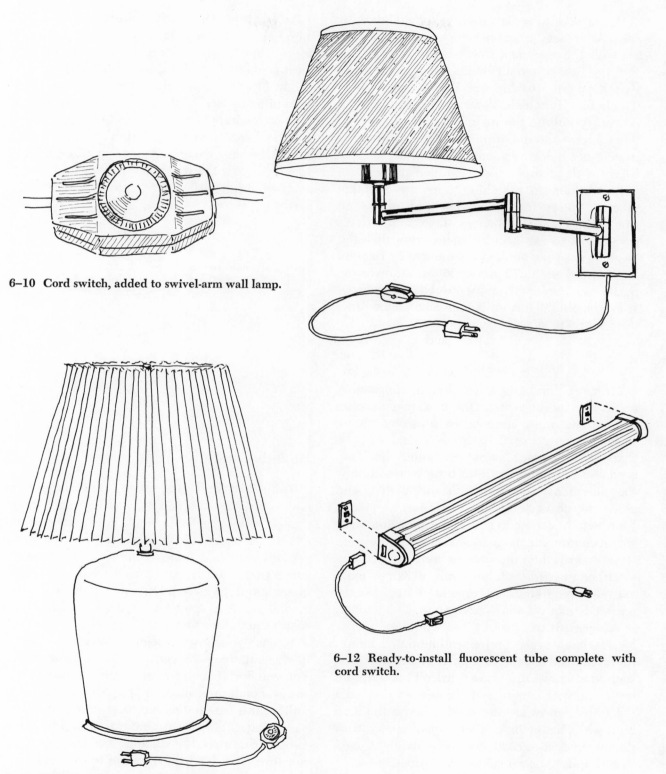

6–10 Cord switch, added to swivel-arm wall lamp.

6–11 Wide-base lamp, less likely to tip over.

6–12 Ready-to-install fluorescent tube complete with cord switch.

If you plan to replace old wall switches with silent switches, remember the rules of safety: Shut off the electric current before you begin. Pull the fuse or circuit breaker that powers the switch you're working on. If you don't know which fuse is which, don't guess; shut off all power by pulling the main switch. Also, if you don't know about wiring terminals inside the switch, get help from someone who does. Electricity is dangerous unless handled properly.

In addition to switches, there are portable plug-in timers for controlling just about all small household appliances. One timer that's convenient to use because of its wide dial and large, easy-to-see numerals is the one by Invento in Figure 6–9 (1,875 watts, ¼ horsepower capacity; 125 volts, 15 amperes; UL approved). It can be obtained from Hammacher Schlemmer for about $13.

Switches at a Distance

No more fumbling about under lampshades for a tiny socket switch; for less than a dollar you can make any lamp easier to use by adding a feed-through cord switch. These can be snapped into place anywhere along the lamp cord and are simple to install. Be sure to follow the directions provided with the switch, and above all, disconnect the lamp before you start. Line switches come in small, medium, and large sizes; choose the large ones because they are easier to grip than the smaller ones.

Although cord switches make all lamps manageable, some kinds of lamp are better for the disabled than others.

Wheelchair users and those who need plenty of clear floor space prefer wall-mounted lamps, especially the ones with a swivel extension arm, such as is shown in Figure 6–10. (This lamp did not come with a cord switch; one was added.)

If table lamps are preferred, choose the kind with wide, heavy bases (see Figure 6–11); they do not tip over as easily as tall lightweight ones. (Here, too, the cord switch was added.)

A lightweight, ready-to-install fluorescent tube, 24 in./610 mm long, is ideal for quickly adding light under a wall cabinet or shelf. A recent innovation by General Electric called Bright Stik, the tube, shown in Figure 6–12, is a completely self-contained fluorescent fixture with no separate bits and pieces to contend with; it comes with the cord switch already in place. When the unit wears out in from three to five years, you toss the whole thing away and install another. Bright Stik costs approximately $14 at hardware stores.

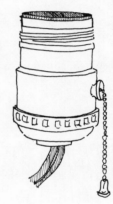

6–13 Pull-chain socket, ideal for the disabled.

Reviving a Relic

Table and wall lamps with pull chains are easier for the disabled to handle than those equipped with socket buttons. Fortunately, pull-chain sockets, old-fashioned as they may be, are still available. Some lamp designers are even using them, too. By all means, look for pull-chain lamps if you're buying new ones, and plan to add them to lamps your disabled friend or relative already owns.

In case you haven't seen a pull-chain socket lately, Figure 6–13 shows what it looks like. You will find it in electrical supply and hardware stores. Some sophisticated lamp designs include pull chains, an indication that true efficiency has no age limit. An example is the brass floor lamp in Figure 6–14, which is available at better furniture and department stores for around $70.

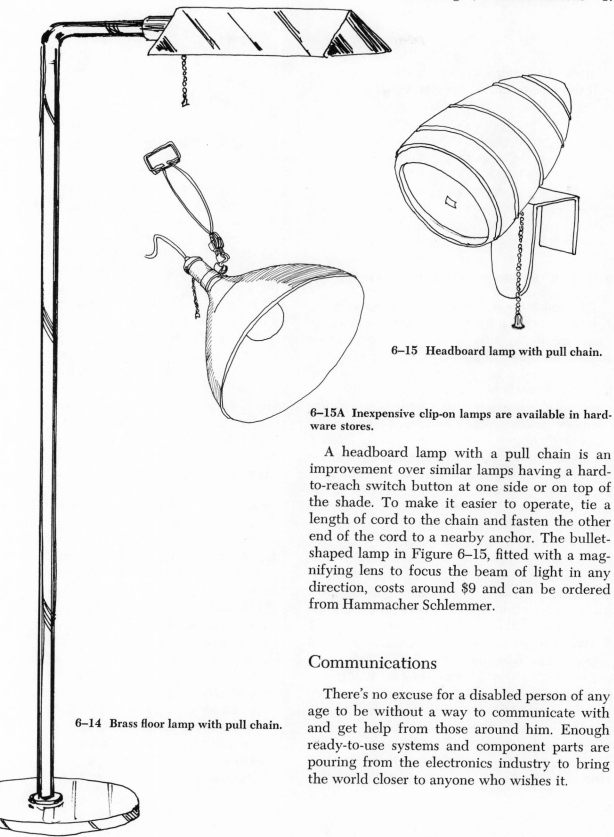

6–15 Headboard lamp with pull chain.

6–15A Inexpensive clip-on lamps are available in hardware stores.

A headboard lamp with a pull chain is an improvement over similar lamps having a hard-to-reach switch button at one side or on top of the shade. To make it easier to operate, tie a length of cord to the chain and fasten the other end of the cord to a nearby anchor. The bullet-shaped lamp in Figure 6–15, fitted with a magnifying lens to focus the beam of light in any direction, costs around $9 and can be ordered from Hammacher Schlemmer.

Communications

There's no excuse for a disabled person of any age to be without a way to communicate with and get help from those around him. Enough ready-to-use systems and component parts are pouring from the electronics industry to bring the world closer to anyone who wishes it.

6–14 Brass floor lamp with pull chain.

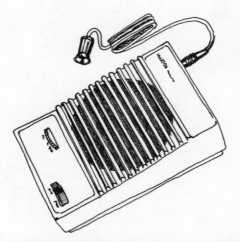

6–16 Telephone amplifier with suction-cup pickup coil.

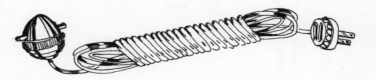

6–17 Extra-long extension cord with remote-control switch.

The Bell System, for one, is continuously involved in creating new ways for the disabled to communicate by way of the home telephone. Indeed, one of the first modifications you should make in a house or apartment for the disabled is a communications system tailored to the person's individual needs. Call your local telephone company business office for information and a copy of their free booklet *Services for Special Needs*. The company's programs and equipment are designed for those with impaired mobility, hearing, or speech.

Citizens' band (CB) radios are another means of communication that happen to be so popular you will have no trouble finding a suitable system. However, for a CB system to work, there must be a responsible person or agency on the other end. Perhaps a neighbor who already has a CB set could help. Local volunteer groups may know of other disabled people who would lend an ear. Also, you could advertise in local papers for a CB buddy.

Built-in intercom systems, once available only for factories and offices, are now made for private homes. From a central control board, one can operate exterior and interior lights, monitor entry doors, and transmit sound from room to room. One such arrangement, by Nutone, can be purchased from larger hardware stores and home electronics shops.

Nowadays you can buy small, inexpensive communicating devices (they're too efficient and useful to be called gadgets) that you install simply by plugging them into a wall outlet. One, by Arista, which you can see on the near right-hand corner of the table in Figure 6–2, is for two-way communication between two rooms (or two buildings, provided both buildings are serviced by a common transformer). An instant-on solid-state unit, it has volume control, a pilot light, and a lock-on switch that doesn't have to be held down during use. No bigger than a ham sandwich, a set of two identical consoles costs about $40. Made by Arista (Model No. 700), it can be ordered from Atlas Electronics Corporation.

The telephone amplifier in Figure 6–16, just one of many kinds available, has a suction-cup pickup coil and a four-transistor circuit. It comes with an on-off switch which locks in place, volume control, and a standard 9-volt battery. Also made by Arista (Model No. 214), it is available from Atlas Electronics Corporation for $16.

Many of the remote-control switch cords currently sold are not as long as you might wish. Often, in order to connect some distant lamp or television set to a switch near a bed or chair, you have to use an assortment of extensions. For neater hookups, a remote on-off cord that's 15 ft./4.5 m long (see Figure 6–17) can be purchased from Atlas Electronics Corporation for about $5. The switch is larger than most and thus easier to grip. This cord is made by Arista (Model No. 451).

6–18 Hooded stake lights to outline ramps and sidewalks.

•

Exterior Lighting

For safety's sake, ramps, sidewalks, and driveways have to be well lighted. In minutes and for less than a hundred dollars, you can install one of the ready-to-go low-voltage (12-volt) systems yourself. Sears, JC Penney, and electrical supply shops sell these as kits, complete with six lights, mounting stakes, and brackets, plus 100 ft./30.4 m of weather-resistant cable and a transformer with automatic timer.

Hooded stake lights, included in the low-voltage kits, are ideal for outlining the route between ramp and sidewalk. Shaded stake lights with long stems are for sidewalks, patios, and shrub and flower borders. They connect into the

6–19 Shaded, long-stem stake lights for patios, steps, and shrubbery.

6–20 Electric-eye floodlights for all-night exterior illumination.

same low-voltage system described, but are sold separately for about $15 each.

For all-night illumination, use electric-eye floodlights which turn on at dusk and off at dawn. These are sold at Sears, JC Penney, and electrical supply stores for about $14, not including bulbs.

Mainstream Source List—Power, Light, Communications

Arista Enterprises, Inc.
Hauppauge, New York 11787

Atlas Electronics Corporation
1570 Third Avenue
New York, New York 10028

Hammacher Schlemmer
147 East 57th Street
New York, New York 10022

Maddak, Inc.
Pequannock, New Jersey 07440

Nutone Division of Scovill
Madison & Red Bank Roads
Cincinnati, Ohio 45227

SGL Waber Electric
300 Harvard Avenue
Westville, New Jersey 08093

Chapter 7

Frustration-Free Storage

Closets, like our own consciences, are holding tanks where we keep all the things we aren't using right now but are bound to need later. Similarly, we tend to keep this baggage of our lives out of sight and often out of reach as well. For the nondisabled—especially the pack rats and compulsive organizers among us—this is a comfortable habit, but an impractical one for those with limited mobility. For them, hanging up a coat, locating a sweater, or replacing a book means spending energy, and this is an unnecessary drain upon already limited reserves. However, just as a heavy spirit is cured by revealing all, so storage accessibility can be improved by removing closet doors and using open shelves instead of drawers.

Openness isn't a rule, though. It's a convenience to be used according to personal preference (the disabled person's). Not everyone is thrilled at the sight of an exposed hall closet. Nor do many people want the contents of their bedroom closet on permanent display. But there are ways to make open storage attractive as well as functional.

The Wherewithal

Up to now, most of the things you've needed to refit the house or apartment have been hard to find, overpriced, or nonexistent. Not so with closets and shelving systems. Everything you'll want to create frustration-free storage is as close as your nearest home center, hardware store, or mail-order catalogue. At reasonable prices, too.

Look for precut and ready-to-assemble shelving with appropriate brackets, supports, rods, and fasteners stocked together for quick selection. Not only do all these components come in a wide variety of sizes, but they are also adjustable—ready and able to fit those strangely shaped nooks and crannies some are pleased to call closets.

Of the three major kinds of closet shelving material you can buy, the most unique is made of open-work steel mesh clad in white nonpeel vinyl. Its related hardware is also vinyl-coated. Precut in lengths of 2 ft./610 mm, 3 ft./914 mm, and 4 ft./1.2 m, the shelves range in depth (front to back) from 9 in./229 mm to 20 in./ 508 mm. They cost about $3 a foot and are made by Closet Maid Corporation.

Adjustable shelves of steel, with baked-on enamel finishes, come in an even wider range of sizes. Those by Stanley, for instance, are 12 in./ 305 mm and 14 in./356 mm deep and are available in seven lengths that adjust from 24 in./ 610 mm to 108 in./2.7 m. Expandable linen-closet shelves are 14 in./356 mm deep and adjust from 18 in./457 mm to 30 in./762 mm or from 30 in./762 mm to 42 in./1.1 m. Prices vary according to shelf size, the smallest being about $8, the largest approximately $30. Some brackets are priced separately, but in general, all fasteners and fittings are included in the shelf price. These are available at Stanley Home Storage Centers in building-supply and hardware stores.

Precut particleboard shelves, in wood-grain or brightly colored vinyl finishes, are among the most inexpensive materials. Prices range from $3.50 for a small 8 × 24 in./203 mm × 610 mm shelf up to $8.00 for one that measures 12 × 48 in./305 mm × 1.2 m. Supports and fasteners must be bought separately; usually slotted metal wall standards with clip-in brackets work well. These allow you to adjust the spacing between shelves. For bright colors—orange, lemon, lime, and white—look for Knape & Vogt's Contemporary Shelf Center at hardware and department stores and some shelf shops.

Fasteners for Safety

About all the tools you'll need to install any of these precut shelves are hammer and screwdriver, although an electric drill would be handy. Above all, use the fastener—screw, nail, or bolt—that's best suited to the kind of wall you are working on, even if it means discarding the ones packaged with the supports and buying others. Anyone with impaired mobility tends to pull downward when retrieving things, so make sure all rods, hooks, and brackets are well anchored right from the beginning. (See "Firm Fastenings" in Chapter 1, pages 11–12.)

Measurements Do Matter

For the disabled, storage anywhere is a blessing as long as it's easy to get to and the contents are within comfortable reach. The following will guide you in refitting and planning new storage places.

SHELVES

Wherever you plan to let shelves do the work of drawers—in room dividers, wall systems, bookcases, or closets—the general rules are these:

Lowest shelf—Should be at least 10 in./254 mm above the floor for adults, proportionately lower for children.

Highest shelf—Should be no more than 48 in./1.2 m above the floor.

Depth (front to back)—Should be no more than 16 in./406 mm. But be guided by what the person can do and by what the shelf will be used for. A book, for example, that extends slightly beyond the edge of its shelf is easy to pull down with one hand, indicating that very shallow bookcases are, for some people, handier than standard-sized ones. This tip comes from Dr. Alice Loomer, post-polio, who is a master at making things work for her rather than the other way around. A record player, on the other hand, needs solid support; a too-narrow shelf would be ridiculous and unsafe.

CLOSETS

Clothes rod—For adult wheelchair users, should be no higher than 48 in./1.2 m above floor.

Storage shelf—Should be 3 in./76 mm above the rod. For children, a clothes rod can be from 30 to 36 in./762 mm to 914 mm above the floor and the shelf 3 in./76 mm above the rod.

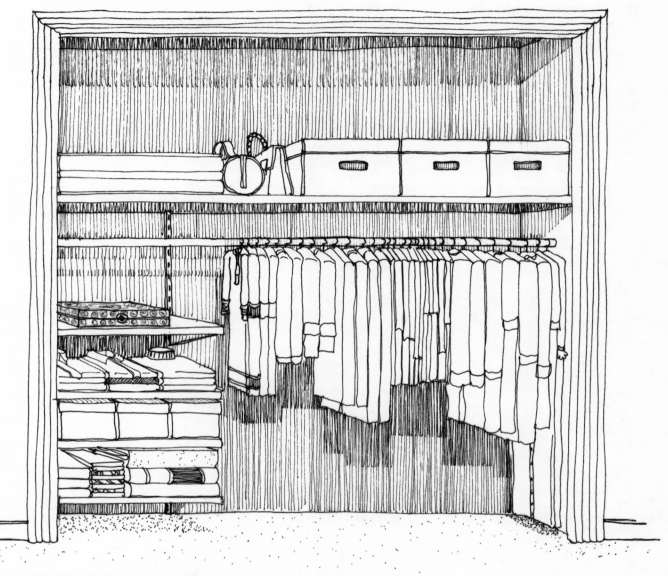

7–1 Ideally, closets for the disabled have no doors, sills, or channel tracks on the floor. Rods, shelves, hooks are all low enough to be reached comfortably.

Surfaces—Whether of shelves or hooks, these should not be slippery but must be smooth. Snags and bumps mean someone has to lift a garment or box; pulling or sliding it would be easier.

Of course, the actual reach of the person, child or adult, is always your best guideline to the placement of anything, no matter where. Find out what the individual's real limits are before you begin a project.

The closet pictured in Figure 7–1 has no door to struggle with, no sill or channel track to bump over. The top shelf and clothes rod are low enough for an adult in a wheelchair to reach comfortably. The shelves at the side are fitted onto adjustable brackets and hold most of the things usually kept in drawers. Light-weight storage boxes and zippered cases on the top shelf can be pulled down by hand or with wood or metal grip extenders. The closet floor is flush with that of the room; no change in level, not even the slightest, exists between the

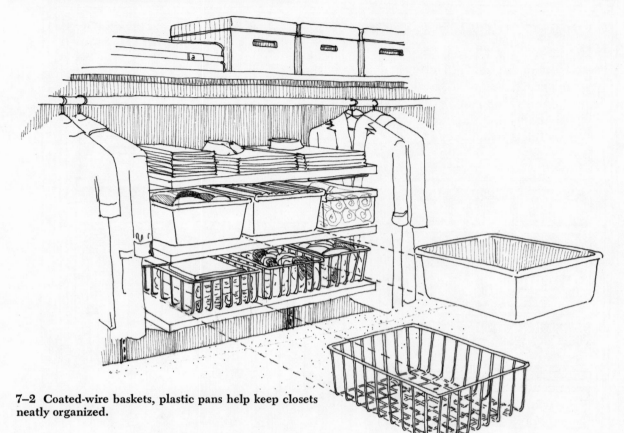

7–2 Coated-wire baskets, plastic pans help keep closets neatly organized.

7–3 Dressing area in a child's bedroom features doorless closet on one wall, grooming shelf and mirror on the other.

two. The hangers are smooth, wide, lightweight plastic or polished wood.

In the closet in Figure 7–2, ordinary plastic dishpans and coated-wire baskets make handy storage containers. They can be filled with items needed daily; things used less frequently can be stored in drawers or on shelves.

The child's closet in Figure 7–3 forms one side of a small dressing area off the bedroom. No doors whatever separate these areas. The shelf under the full-width mirror and fluorescent lighting on the opposite wall is for grooming aids when the child is older.

Doors

Of course you will want doors on some closets. You have only to decide what kind.

Bifold doors are one choice. There are sizes to fit standard openings, and the hardware can be surface-mounted. When open, bifold doors reveal all or nearly all of the interior, making the contents more accessible. However, because there are two, getting these doors open requires more motion than opening others. But bifolds demand less reach and operate smoothly. They are also light in weight.

Bifold doors should fit loosely so as not to bind, but be installed firmly enough to stay in proper balance. Replace small knobs with handles suited to the person's grasp: D-shaped wood or metal, levers, pulls of leather, rope, cloth, yarns.

Sliding doors are suitable for persons with good upper-torso strength, provided you use lightweight ones. Look for the inexpensive kind made mostly of cardboard. After all, closet doors are not meant to control noise, merely the view.

Select low-priced doors, but buy good hardware. If this seems a bit impractical, just consider: manipulating sliding doors from a seated position or with weak arms is not easy under any conditions. Why add to the struggle with doors that bind and drag? Instead, reduce the

7–4 Bifold closet doors, suitable for individuals with good balance and a well-coordinated hand and arm.

effort by using better-grade aluminum track, a floating suspension-top hanger, nylon floor glides. You will find sliding-door hardware in mail-order catalogues, home centers, and large hardware stores. Cut handholds all the way through the doors or replace recessed pulls with leather or cloth straps.

Draw draperies on a ceiling track have possibilities you may not have thought of in connection with closets. They take up almost no space, fit any size opening, weigh very little, and give full-width accessibility to what is stored behind them. What's more, they're easy to open and close with one hand while standing or sitting in one position.

Use window-drapery hardware, of course, but buy the best to assure an operating mechanism that works smoothly. Also, let the pull cord be on a tension bracket that's mounted on the wall about 2 ft./610 mm above floor level. Fasten it

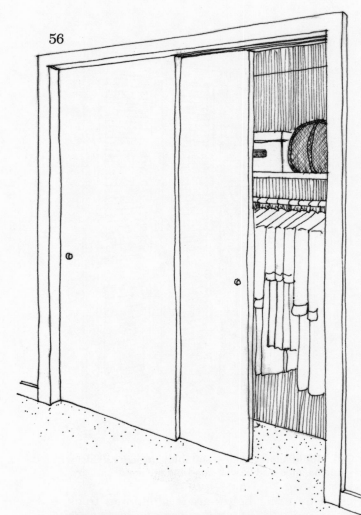

7–5 Sliding closet doors, suitable for those with good strength in upper torso, coordinated hand and arm.

securely. And be sure there is enough space at the side of the pull-cord bracket to accommodate anyone in a wheelchair or on crutches.

Open Storage

No matter what you do to make closets more accessible, they won't be as convenient, or labor-saving, as flexible systems of shelves and open cubes that you set up anywhere. Buy entire systems ready-made or make them yourself. They can be expensive or cheap; have high style or no style; be made of almost anything old or new—wood, metal, plastic, cardboard, particleboard.

Convenience Comes First

How many "storage stations" to have and where to put them depends upon the person who'll use them. Strive for convenience; have as many as it takes to save him or her from making unnecessary moves. Duplicate contents where reasonable. For instance, have keys, scarves, gloves, sunglasses, combs, mirrors, makeup, and the like in several locations.

Be guided also by the physical capabilities of the person who uses this kind of open storage. Understand the extent of his or her grasp strength. Be aware of the energy drain likely to be involved in bending, turning, or standing. Adjust shelf levels and depths accordingly.

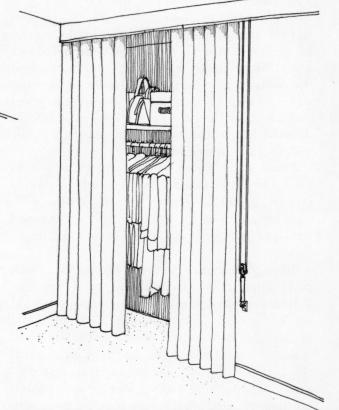

7–6 Draw draperies cover closet opening; add wall-mounted pull-cord bracket with clear "parking space" on its approach side.

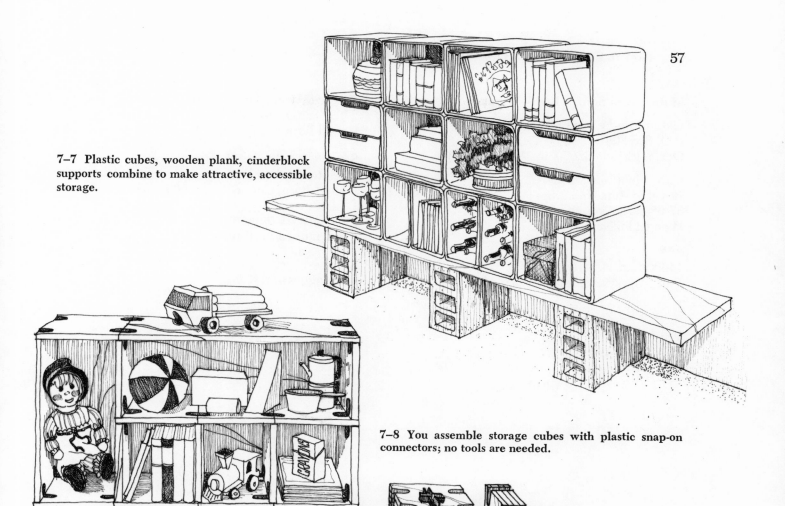

7–7 Plastic cubes, wooden plank, cinderblock supports combine to make attractive, accessible storage.

7–8 You assemble storage cubes with plastic snap-on connectors; no tools are needed.

Style, Too

If it seems to you that convenience is so important style must suffer in the process, be cheered. There are so many well-designed components available today that open storage, like a salad, can be concocted for any taste. Here are just two examples from hundreds of possibilities. They are attractive, functional, and easy to do yourself.

In Figure 7–7, plastic cubes are grouped together on a thick wooden plank supported by plain ordinary cinder block. Other supports could be bricks, flue tile, patterned cement blocks, even wall-mounted braces to hold the unit completely off the floor. Strips of thin

double-faced tape between the cubes hold them securely to each other. Cubes are available everywhere and come in expensive plastics or less costly composition board or particleboard. Those shown are 13½ in./343 mm square; other sizes, smaller as well as larger, are to be found.

See Figure 7–8 for squares and rectangles of wood that become cubes when you fit them together with plastic connectors. You do it by hand (no tools needed), much like a jigsaw puzzle. There's almost no limit to what the possibilities are. Build as high as the person can reach, as long as the space permits; form right angles or make steplike configurations. The lowest shelf here, for a child, is 6 in./152 mm above the floor. This system is Cubex by Cado, available from Royal System, Inc.

Mainstream Source List—Storage

Closet Maid Corporation
P.O. Box 304
Ocala, Florida 32670

Cubex by Cado
Royal System, Inc.
57-08 39th Avenue
Woodside, New York 11377

AND

14600 Lanark Street
Van Nuys, California 91402

Knape & Vogt Manufacturing Co.
2700 Oak Drive N.E.
Grand Rapids, Michigan 49505

Stanley Hardware Division
The Stanley Works
New Britain, Connecticut 06050

JC Penney Company
Catalogues and stores

Sears
Catalogues and stores

Chapter 8

Furniture and Room Arrangement

If you suppose, as many nondisabled persons do, that the disabled or elderly need hospital-like surroundings, know that just the opposite is true.

All the old familiar chairs, tables, beds, sofas, and lamps will do nicely just as they are, or if not quite right, can be easily adapted to suit a changed life-style. What's more, they are not just pieces of furniture any more but symbols of freedom, tools the disabled will use to create an atmosphere of independence that would be impossible in an institutional environment.

Some special equipment for improving the person's mobility and capacity to function will be necessary, of course—wheelchair, crutches, lifts. But these are separate entities, detachable and apart from the elements of personal style that stamp a private dwelling place as one's own.

To reinforce a sense of belonging, it is important to the disabled that you preserve the familiar characteristics of a home and make changes only to improve its safety and accessibility.

One of the simplest ways to do this is by rearranging the furniture. The arrangement you choose should provide clear and direct routes through one room to another. It should also make moving from place to place within the room as effortless as possible.

Let the size of the room determine where the furniture will go. If it's small, arrange the pieces around the edge of the room. Leave the center open for traffic flow.

Alice Loomer, a post-polio who moves about her city apartment in a motorized chair, prefers having the center of the room open because that's what works best for her. She says, "A room should have no inaccessible spots. I should be able to go anywhere in it." For visitors to Dr. Loomer's apartment, there are comfortable sofas and chairs. Several small occasional chairs are on casters. "They are easy to push out of the way

8–1 An attractive living room, yet comfortably accessible. Furniture groupings (A) allow wide aisles in and through this living room.

when I don't need them. I put casters on just about everything," she says.

A large room would look awkward and uninviting if all the furniture were pushed against the walls. For such rooms, center islands of furniture, flanked by clear passageways—4 to 5 ft./1.2 to 1.5 m wide—along the perimeter would be better.

An accessible room, yet one containing all the

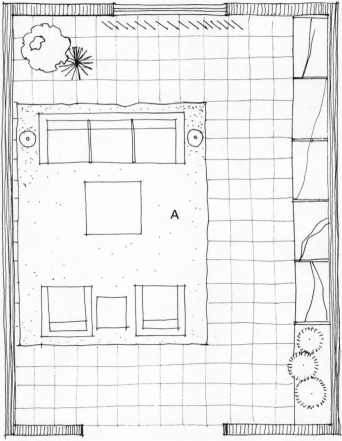

elements everyone likes a living room to have, is illustrated in Figure 8–1. Sofa, chairs, table, lamps, desk, bookcases, storage, plants, and pictures are all arranged in a pleasing but compact way. A smooth, dense, low-level pile area rug has no padding under it to reduce the annoying ridge that wheelchairs would have to bump over. Bookcases, storage unit, and drop-front desk along one wall can be adjusted to any height on the supporting uprights. The same

arrangement could also be wall-mounted, leaving the floor beneath free of any obstructions. Period and traditional furniture would look equally well in an arrangement like this one.

Bedrooms can be functional yet attractive, too. Simplicity, convenience, and color are the key. Scatter or area rugs should never be used; the floor should be left entirely bare, or else have wall-to-wall carpeting, even in the closet. Getting dressed and groomed is a chore for the

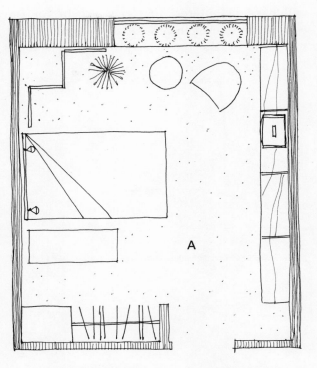

8–2 Bedroom is functional, yet cozy. Note casters on bedside table, wicker furniture for guests. Situate bed so that sides are accessible (A); arrange storage pieces at comfortable heights.

another as accent color. Avoid drab, monotonous colors and large, busy patterns. In Figure 8–2, a bedside control center (see Chapter 6) is arrayed on a long, narrow Parsons table fitted with large ball casters.

Chairs to Have

In general, the top surface of a chair seat should be 18 in./457 mm above floor level, but your friend or relative may be more comfortable with a height that is more or less than this average. To adjust a chair's height, consider cutting down the legs or building them up on blocks or a platform. Add a thicker seat cushion only as a last resort, since that would not only change the lines of the chair but cause the chair arms to be lower, hence not very comfortable.

Anyone who uses a wheelchair all the time

disabled; keeping the floor as smooth as possible helps make the necessary moving about less arduous. The bed should be situated so that the sides are accessible for getting in and out of, and for bed making. Tables on casters are easily pushed out of the way when necessary. Drawer and cabinet storage can be arranged together along one wall opposite the bed. As for a room's color scheme, plan it around the person's favorites; use one color as the dominant hue, and

will have no interest in chairs except for the comfort of guests and as suitable elements in a room's decor. But the elderly and those who use

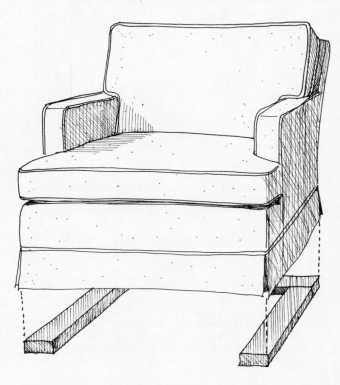

8–3 Elevate low chairs with homemade U-shaped platforms.

crutches, braces, prostheses, or canes or who move from wheelchair to stationary chair are definitely concerned, especially about the chair's stability and seat height. These people tend to approach a chair, then turn, back up, and literally fall into it. Therefore, no casters or slippery glides! The chair must remain firmly in place. Also, the chair seat should be higher than usual—so there's not so far to "fall"—and the seat itself should be firm, not squashy.

Don't think you have to throw out any chair that does not fit these requirements. It's easy enough to raise an existing chair to proper height.

Modern lounge chairs are usually quite low (to conform to contemporary interior design)

but can be made higher, nevertheless. Since a thicker seat cushion would alter line and proportion, it would be better to raise the whole chair on a homemade U-shaped platform (see Figure 8–3). Leave the platform open in front to allow toe space, and paint it to match a dominant color in either the upholstery or carpet. To hold the chair in place on the platform, you can drive a nail through the bottom of the platform straight into the center of each chair leg. Or you could fasten rubber furniture cups to the platform (with glue or nails) and place the chair legs in them.

Reclining chairs are usually firm and sturdily built, and are not apt to skid out from under someone trying to get in or out of them. But if the seat is not quite high enough for the person who's to use it, elevate the whole chair on a U-shaped platform. Recliners are widely available in stores and from mail order houses.

Upholstered chairs sold as office furnishings

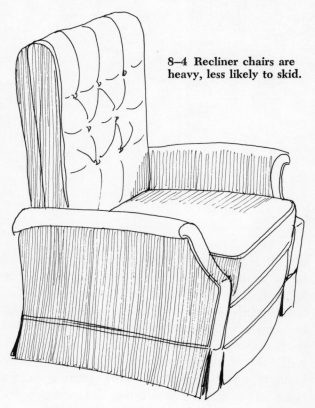

8–4 Recliner chairs are heavy, less likely to skid.

are excellent for those who have difficulty getting up and sitting down, since they are heavier and higher than most living-room chairs. However, their most outstanding feature is the firm padding which is typical of such furniture. Look for these in the Yellow Pages under Office Furnishings.

Chairs with swivel seats are also excellent for those who are partially ambulatory, provided the chair is well supported on firm legs. (Avoid swivel chairs that also rock; they're tricky to get in and out of.) One of the best swivel-seat chairs is the solid pine captain's chair which you buy in kit form for $70 (you assemble, stain and finish it yourself), or order fully finished for $90. Wooden legs can be cut down or added to if height has to be adjusted. Chairs or kits are available by mail order from Yield House.

Desks and Tables

Drop-front desks and those with wide knee-space openings are best for wheelchair users. As a rule, the top surface should be 32 in./813 mm above floor level and have a clearance of 29½ in./749 mm between the floor and the underside of the surface. This permits wheelchair armrests to fit under the desk or table top. Also, wheelchair users and others need an open front-to-back depth of at least 24 in./610 mm under desks and tables for their feet and legs.

Desks and tables with a front cutout are especially comfortable for many disabled children and adults. The wrap-around offers extra support for arms and shoulders, and makes books, papers, and the like easier to reach. Very few tables or desks are designed this way, but you can create a wrap-around work surface on almost any table or flat-topped desk by attaching a plywood top with a front cutout, as has been done in Figure 8–6.

This Parsons table is 18 in./457 mm deep, 36 in./914 mm long, and 30 in./762 mm high. Attached to its solid wood top is a cutout top

8–5 Office-furniture chairs are high, firmly upholstered.

made of ¾ in./19 mm plywood that measures 20 in./508 mm deep by 36 in./914 mm long. This permits a 7 in./179 mm overhang and a 5 in./127 mm wide recess along the back of the table for setting in a row of inexpensive wicker letter holders. A hobby table or personal dining table can be made the same way. The plywood top can be painted, stained, or covered in colorful paper, fabric, vinyl, stick-on carpet tiles, or resilient vinyl floor tiles. Table height can be adjusted by cutting legs down, attaching blocks, or fitting with casters.

Most dining and work tables are constructed with a fascia or apron support under the top which prevents wheelchair armrests from fitting under the table, thus limiting a close approach. Occasionally tables are made without these small obstructions, but you could spend weeks trying to find a suitable one. It will save time and money to make the right kind of table yourself by fitting a wood, glass, or particleboard top with legs that you can buy separately at mail-

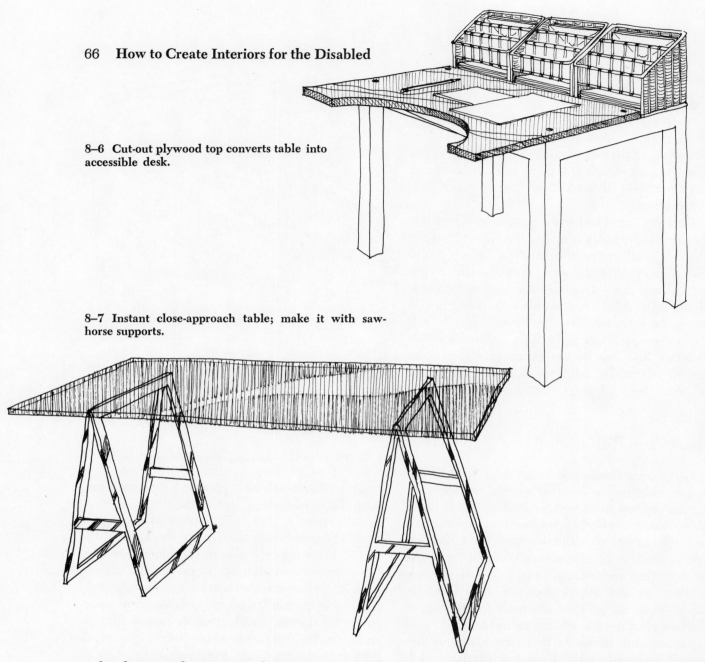

8–6 Cut-out plywood top converts table into accessible desk.

8–7 Instant close-approach table; make it with saw-horse supports.

order houses, door stores, home centers, and hardware stores.

For a sophisticated touch, a table such as the one in Figure 8–7 could be made of thick plate glass laid over two polished chrome sawhorses. (Avoid glass unless the person is well coordinated and naturally cautious. Butcher block or other wood planking would do just as well.) Sawhorse bases are available through designers and are sold in better furniture and decorative-accessory shops.

A solid butcher-block top can be fastened to turned-wood end supports (see Figure 8–8). A solid flush door would also make a satisfactory top. Wood legs are sold in large hardware stores and in home centers.

Particleboard cut in round, square, or rectangular shapes can be fitted with plain metal pipe legs. If you paint the top or cover it with fabric, vinyl, or stick-on floor tiles, who's going to know you made the whole thing for less than thirty dollars?

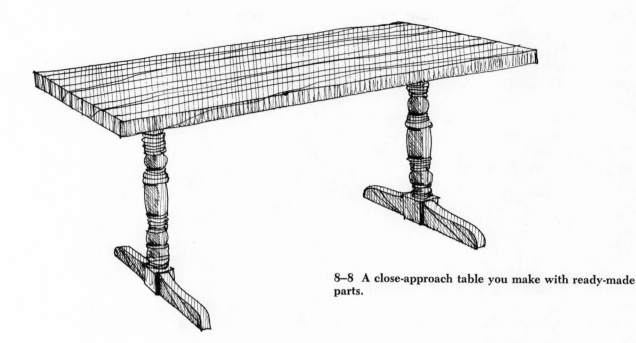

8–8 A close-approach table you make with ready-made parts.

All About Beds

There should be at least 3½ ft./1,066 mm of space between the side of the bed and the wall or other pieces of furniture, so that the disabled person has ample room to transfer to and from bed and wheelchair.

Suit the height of the bed—the distance from the top surface of the mattress to the floor—to the person who will be using it. For wheelchair users, the top of the mattress should be level with the wheelchair seat, so that the transfer from one to the other can be made with as little effort as possible.

For anyone who has difficulty standing up or sitting down, the bed should be raised or lowered to whatever height the person needs. Wooden and metal beds can be raised on wooden blocks. If the bed needs to be lowered, and it's made of wood, simply saw portions of the legs off. If the frame is metal, all you can do is switch the mattress and box spring to a wooden frame and adjust accordingly. Some-

times casters will raise a bed to exactly the desired level. If you do plan to use them, get the kind with brakes. If your hardware store does not have this kind in stock, have a set ordered for you.

If you use wooden blocks to raise a bed to some desired level, be sure the blocks are thick and heavy and that the legs of the bed are securely fitted into the blocks; a rickety arrangement could pull loose or cause the bed to tip over. Drill or chisel out deep recesses in the blocks to fit the bed legs into.

Beds for the disabled should have headboards—to prop against, hang on to, pull on. Make sure the headboard is sturdy; strength, in this instance, is more important than style. For some, a footboard will be handy, too. A rope or pulley arrangement can be attached to it—provided the bed is sturdily built. Blankets and top sheet can be draped over the footboard to relieve pressure on feet and toes.

Motorized beds are available from medical supply houses and some specialized retail stores. These can supply the complete unit—headboard, frame, mechanical unit, and mattress—or the mechanical unit alone. Either way, prices are high: from $400 for the motorized section to $700 or more for a complete bed. Prices vary between retail outlets and the medical supply houses, so shop both before you buy. Ask the rehab team for the names of at least two medical supply places so you can compare their prices. One retail store that regularly stocks motorized beds is Hammacher Schlemmer in New York City.

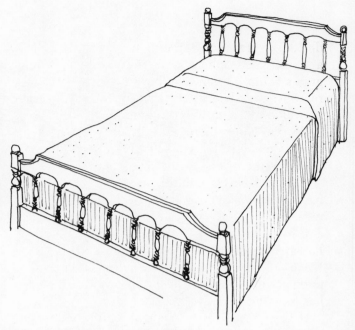

Mattress and Bedding

From the Institute of Rehabilitation Medicine, New York University Medical Center, comes this good advice about bedding: whether foam, hair, or innerspring, mattresses should be firm. A doctor may, for medical reasons, recommend a foam mattress of a certain thickness; in most instances, it can be put on top of the existing mattress.

As for mattress pads, use the slipover kind that fully encases top, sides, and ends. This sort of pad is less likely to wrinkle under the person lying in bed.

Use contoured bottom sheets because they tend to stay more firmly in place. Choose cotton sheets instead of synthetic ones, which are likely

8–9 For some disabled, beds with sturdy footboards and headboards are essential.

to be slippery. Extra-large blankets and top sheets will reduce pressure on toes and be less likely to pull out of place.

Floors and Floor Coverings

Whether floors should be bare, fully covered, or partially covered is a matter of personal preference. If the disabled man or woman lives alone, then it's strictly up to that individual to

8–10 Motorized beds today need not look institutional.

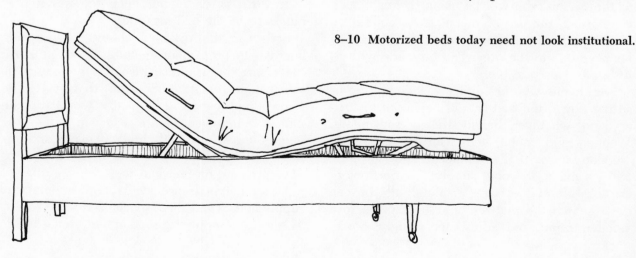

decide. Some people prefer the warmth, color, and soft atmosphere that rugs and carpeting give a room. Others like bare floors for various reasons: they like the look of wood or they feel bare floors are easier to maintain.

People who use crutches, braces, and the like often want some kind of soft covering underfoot; it makes them less apt to slip.

Although it's generally assumed that hard, bare floors are best for wheelchairs, not all wheelchair users agree; many want carpeting and have it. Claire Scholz, for one, says, "We've had our house fully carpeted because we like the homelike atmosphere it gives. I may be stuck in this dumb chair, but that's no reason this place has to look institutional."

If the decision is in favor of wall-to-wall carpeting, choose one with a dense low-level pile. Have a thin but firm padding underneath or have no padding at all. Wheeling across a soft, plushy floor is just as difficult as driving a car in sand. In fact, foam-backed carpet and carpet tile are excellent floor coverings. They're firm, smooth, easy to install.

Room-size rugs and area rugs are acceptable unless they are so plushy or thickly padded that they create a ledge which someone could trip over or have trouble crossing.

Wood and resilient vinyl floors are also fine if they are coated with a nonslip finish and never waxed.

Avoid, absolutely, deep-pile carpeting and shaggy shag rugs. And never have scatter rugs anywhere, ever.

Mainstream Source List—Furniture

Hammacher Schlemmer
147 East 57th Street
New York, New York 10022

Yield House
North Conway, New Hampshire 03860

Chapter 9

Bathrooms and Fixtures

Even if we all had the agility of an Olympic gymnast, the twentieth-century bathroom would still be the least safe, most inadequately designed, poorest-furnished space inside the human habitat. Coping with its slippery, hard surfaces and jutting shapes is a daily challenge for the nondisabled, so you can imagine the strain this room imposes on anyone who is permanently or temporarily disabled.

But it's useless to take time listing the wrongs of bathrooms and fixtures. People have been doing that for years, and nothing has changed. If you're building from scratch or remodeling extensively, there are ways to build in more safety, convenience, and space with such recently developed new products as flexible shower attachments and the molded fiberglass roll-in shower with graded entry ramp.

Making a suitable bathroom out of an existing one poses several problems, some of which can be solved without too much effort and expense. Lack of adequate floor space, however, is one that has no solution if the disabled person depends entirely upon a wheelchair to move about.

Wheelchair users need 5 ft./1.5 m of turning space inside the bathroom. Doorways should have flush sills and a clear opening of 30 to 32 in./762 to 813 mm. For constant wheelchair users, a bathroom without these dimensional features must be considered inaccessible until extensive renovations are made, such as widening the door and relocating some of the fixtures.

On the other hand, if the person can stand, even briefly, or transfer from one chair outside the bathroom to another one inside it (a shower chair or a typist's chair, for example), a small bathroom with too-narrow door may be made to work. If you decide on such a solution, install grab bars on the inside *and* outside of the doorframe. Just be sure the bars are securely fastened with the proper bolts or screws because they will be subjected to enormous weight and pull. A bathroom light switch installed outside the bathroom would be a great help, too.

Problems with existing bathrooms start at the threshold, and since everything about this room needs attention, one might as well begin at the door and proceed inside from there.

Doors and Doorways

It's already been stated that sills should be flush and the doorway wide enough to permit passage of a wheelchair. To save space inside the bathroom, the door should swing outward. Most do not, and besides there's usually not enough room in the approaching hallway to accommodate an outward-opening door. Folding doors are one solution.

Another is the remedy found by Al and Claire Scholz. They suspended a plain, unadorned flush door, 36 in./914 mm wide, on a wall-mounted overhead track. At the lightest touch, it will roll completely over the opening or slide to the side of the opening when not needed. The key to this kind of efficiency is the track hardware, which Al finally found after a long search. It is the Deluxe By-Pass Wardrobe Hardware track by Johnson Hardware Products, Inc., Series 2600F, Size 96 inch. The price: $20. The flush door cost $24 dollars. Al Scholz did the installation.

Sinks and Lavatories

These present special problems because they don't project out far enough to permit close approach for wheelchairs. Furthermore, if they are low enough to reach across comfortably, the bowl and drain will be in the way. If they are high enough to obviate this objection, nothing is accessible. The best solution is the wheelchair sink, a sleek wedge of white vitreous china with curved front and a drain offset at the back. It projects outward 27 in./686 mm from the wall and is just 20 in./508 mm wide. Your plumber can order it for you and must install it according to local safety codes. It's the Morningside No. K-12635, by Kohler.

Wristblade faucets are attractive as well as functional. They extend outward and have flat, wide, winglike ends which can be pushed with forearm, wrist, or heel of the hand. Figure 9–1

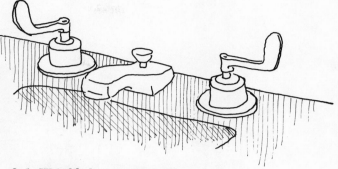

9–1 Wristblade control handles.

shows wristblade control handles (4 in./102 mm) with faucet, aerator, and pop-up drain (No. K-13346 by Kohler). There's also a 5 in./125 mm wristblade control handle (not shown) that can be used in combination with any one of three concealed faucets in the 8100 Olympian series by Bradley; ask for wristblade control handle No. 8105.

Free-standing bathroom sinks should have extra support since the disabled tend to lean heavily on the front edge. Support brackets similar to those in Figure 9–2 can be found in hardware stores and plumbing supply shops. By all means install such supports if you notice that

9–2 Support brackets for bathroom sink.

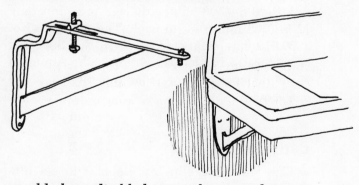

an elderly or disabled person has a tendency to depend upon the sink for leverage.

Counter-top sinks or lavatories are the best solution to problems of support and access. Counter-tops also provide within-reach storage for the many items usually kept in a medicine cabinet, which is always inaccessible to anyone

9–3 Small Spacelyn lavatory by American Standard.

seated in a wheelchair.

If space is a problem, perhaps one of the smaller lavatories would do, such as the Spacelyn, by American Standard, in Figure 9–3. The sink is 20 in./508 mm across and measures only 12 in./305 mm front to back. The Spacelyn No. 3220.019 has right-side fittings; the Spacelyn No. 3222.015 has left-side fittings; the Aquarian II single-lever control (sold separately) is the one shown.

Bathtubs

They are hard, slippery, difficult to get into and out of. But there are ways to make them more accessible, comfortable, and safe. For the disabled, one of the best things to come along since sliced bread is the flexible shower attachments now widely available in stores and from catalogues.

The attachment shown in Figure 9–4 (A)

allows a conventional shower head to be used when desired, and holds a personal shower head that can be lifted from a wall bracket placed at any location near the bather. A diverter (B) with a control button at the side directs water flow through either the conventional shower head or the personal one. Sears Add-A-Shower, Model No. 356.20431.

One of the most versatile systems for new construction as well as remodeling is the Raindrop Personal Shower from Kohler (see Figure 9–5):

A. Rite-Temp pressure balance mixing valve maintains desired water temperature regardless of pressure changes in the water supply (No. K-6913).

B. Raindrop model No. K-9652 has a chrome-plated tub diverter spout and comes with two acrylic wall brackets.

C. Model No. K-9650 allows direct attachment to

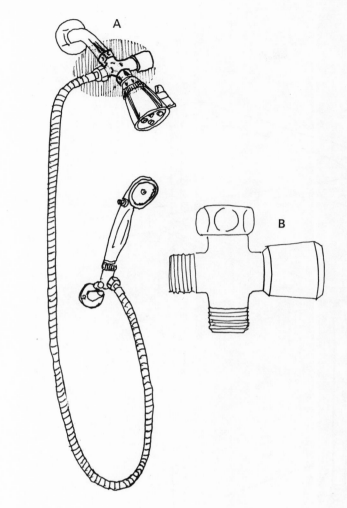

9–4 **Flexible shower attachment (A) and water-flow diverter (B) for shower attachments, both from Sears.**

 shower arm and comes with two acrylic wall brackets.

D. Model No. K-9654 with a chrome-plated 24 in./610 mm slide bar, acrylic adjusting knob, and swivel hanger. A two-way diverter valve (No. K-9662) can be added to permit use of a conventional shower head.

 Bathtub furnishings and furniture help make bathing somewhat more comfortable and safe. An example is the inside-outside transfer bench shown in Figure 9–6. It has adjustable legs and nonslip rubber tips, and is available from Whitaker's for about $63 (model No. 660).

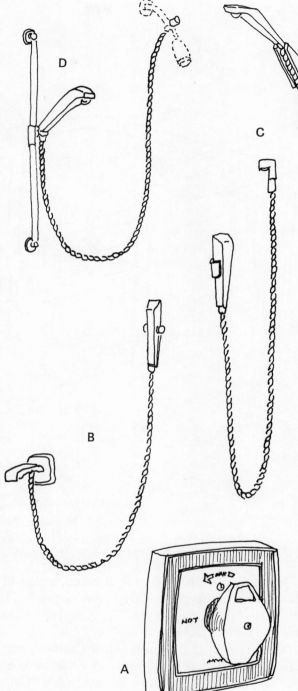

9–5 **The Raindrop Personal Shower, from Kohler: (A) Rite-Temp mixing valve; (B) tub diverter spout; (C) shower arm attachment; (D) slide bar and diverter.**

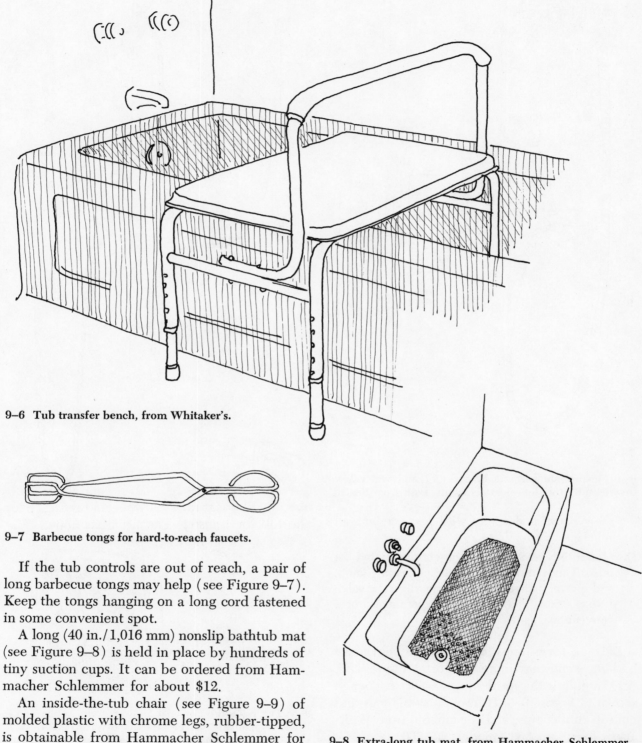

9–6 Tub transfer bench, from Whitaker's.

9–7 Barbecue tongs for hard-to-reach faucets.

If the tub controls are out of reach, a pair of long barbecue tongs may help (see Figure 9–7). Keep the tongs hanging on a long cord fastened in some convenient spot.

A long (40 in./1,016 mm) nonslip bathtub mat (see Figure 9–8) is held in place by hundreds of tiny suction cups. It can be ordered from Hammacher Schlemmer for about $12.

An inside-the-tub chair (see Figure 9–9) of molded plastic with chrome legs, rubber-tipped, is obtainable from Hammacher Schlemmer for

9–8 Extra-long tub mat, from Hammacher Schlemmer.

9–9 Tub chair, from Hammacher Schlemmer.

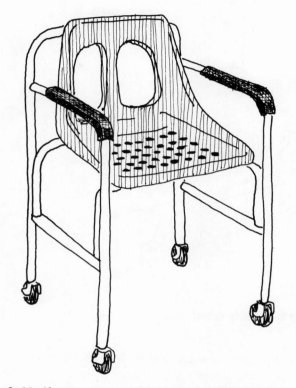

9–11 Shower chair on wheels, from Nelson Medical.

about $30. The back is 28 in./711 mm high; the seat is 15 in./381 mm high and 19 in./483 mm wide (side to side).

The Hoyer Bath Lift in Figure 9–10 uses no electricity, but operates hydraulically with water pressure from a special faucet that comes with the lift. The seat raises, lowers, and swings over the tub for transfer. The lift costs about $320 and is available from MED, Inc.

Showers

Conventional stall showers are too small for wheelchair users and the high step-over lip at the entrance is difficult for others to manage. Until recently, wide roll-in showers had to be custom-built. Now, the Braun Corporation has created a molded fiberglass ready-to-install unit that is 4½ ft./1.4 m square. A graded entry-and-

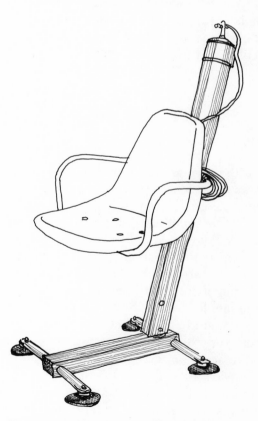

9–10 Hoyer Bath Lift, from MED, Inc.

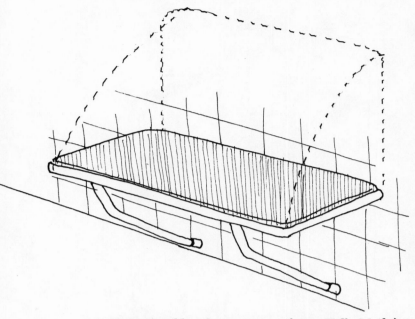

9–12 Retractable shower seat, from Hall Mack/ NuTone.

exit lip assures accessibility by wheelchair, yet keeps water from running out. This is available as a one-piece unit for $525, or in two pieces (for easier installation) for $625. Doors, shower

9–13 Elevated toilet seat attachment, from Nelson Medical.

fittings, and the like are extra. Write the Braun Corporation for product and shipping information.

A precast terrazzo shower floor with a wheelchair threshold is available for builders and home remodelers. The floor slopes gently downward from a floor-level entry lip to a center drain. It comes in five sizes, the largest being 42 in./1,067 mm deep (front to back) and 54 in./1.4 m wide. Prices and shipping requirements vary, so write Creative Industries, Inc., for information.

A molded plastic chair such as the one in Figure 9–11 makes it easier to get around inside the bathroom and shower. This chair, on 3 in./ 76 mm casters, is only 21 in./533 mm wide and can therefore be a big help inside a small, cramped bathroom. It is available for about $85 from Nelson Medical Products. A retractable shower seat is ideal where space is limited. A seat made of tubular stainless steel, with a foam-rubber cushion covered in off-white Naugahyde, can be obtained for about $140 from Hall Mack Division, NuTone Housing Products (see Figure 9–12).

Toilets

Often the turn-around space needed in bathrooms for wheelchair users is blocked by the base of a floor-mounted toilet. Also, for many disabled, the toilet seat is too low. A wall-mounted toilet would solve both problems. If most other features about the bathroom are favorable, it would be worthwhile replacing the existing fixture with the new one. If you rent, the landlord may be willing to permit the exchange; consult a plumber and get prices so that you and the property owner or manager can arrive at a fair agreement.

Other ways to make an existing toilet more comfortable and convenient are the many seat attachments and handrail safety frames now available.

The portable elevated toilet seat in Figure 9–13 adjusts from 4 to 8 in./102 to 203 mm on padded steel support brackets. It fits all standard toilets. It is available, complete with one-piece splash guard, from Nelson Medical Products for $27 with a white enameled seat and for $35 with a padded seat.

Three inches (76 mm) higher than conventional floor-mounted toilets is the 18 in./457 mm model (No. K-3518-EB), shown in Figure 9–14. A specially designed seat with securely attached supporting arms can be added. The seat with arms is sold separately; ask for model No. K-4655. Both are by Kohler.

Slip-over toilet guardrails can easily be attached to any toilet on one or both sides. Those in Figure 9–15 are of chrome-plated tubular steel with plastic armrests and nonskid feet, and can be obtained for $18 from Nelson Medical Products.

In judging toilet accessibility, take into account how the disabled person must mount the toilet: from right or left side or from the front.

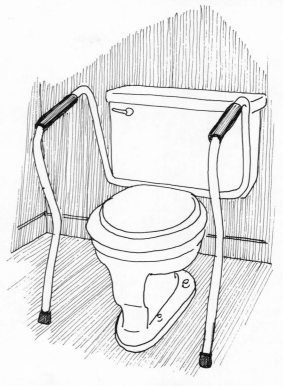

9–15 Slip-over guardrails, from Nelson Medical.

If a side approach is indicated (members of the rehab team should tell you), the toilet will have to be situated—or relocated—to permit this. It's best to know what's needed before the person comes home so you will have time to make the bathroom more convenient.

Storage

There's never enough storage space in bathrooms anyway, and with the extra guardrails and personal hygiene aids the disabled need, there'll be even less. Add narrow shelves where you can; hang coated-wire racks and baskets at convenient levels for toiletries, towels, facecloths, and other supplies. Recessed medicine cabinets above sinks are inaccessible to anyone who is seated, but you could hang one on the back of a door or on a wall if there's space. Otherwise, add a shallow shelf over the sink or alongside it.

9–14 Extra-high toilet and seat-with-arms (sold separately), by Kohler.

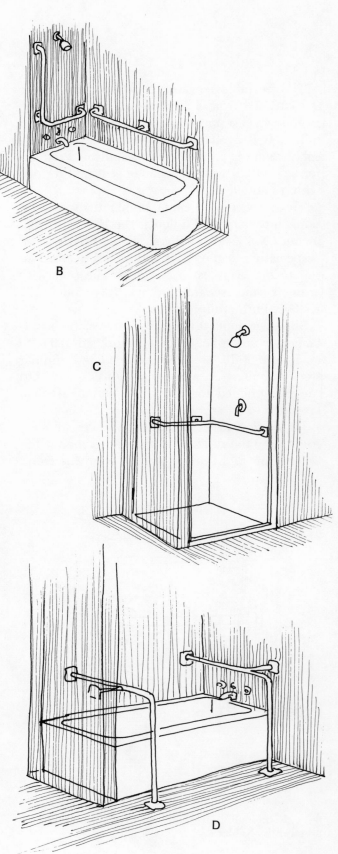

9–16 Grab bars are a must; here are some ways to use them: (A) wall-to-floor installation; (B) angle-bar and straight bar; (C) right-handed angle bar; (D) wall-to-floor with wall posts.

•

Supports for Safety

Where firm, solid support is needed—and where is it more important than in bathrooms? —don't stint. Institutional-grade stainless steel grab bars are made for residential use, thank goodness, and though expensive, will be worth it in the long run. Towel bars are no substitute for safety bars. Moreover, grab bars should not be used as towel bars, either; one frantic grasp for a support that's covered with a towel, and both towel and hand will slip off. Pay the price for well-made bars, put them wherever they are necessary (see examples in Figure 9–16), and follow the maker's directions for secure installation TO THE LETTER. There's almost no size or configuration you could think up that hasn't been made. Figure 9–17 shows only a few from Hall Mack. You'd be wise to look over the full range before you make any decisions. Write for the NuTone–Hall Mack Bath Accessories catalogue.

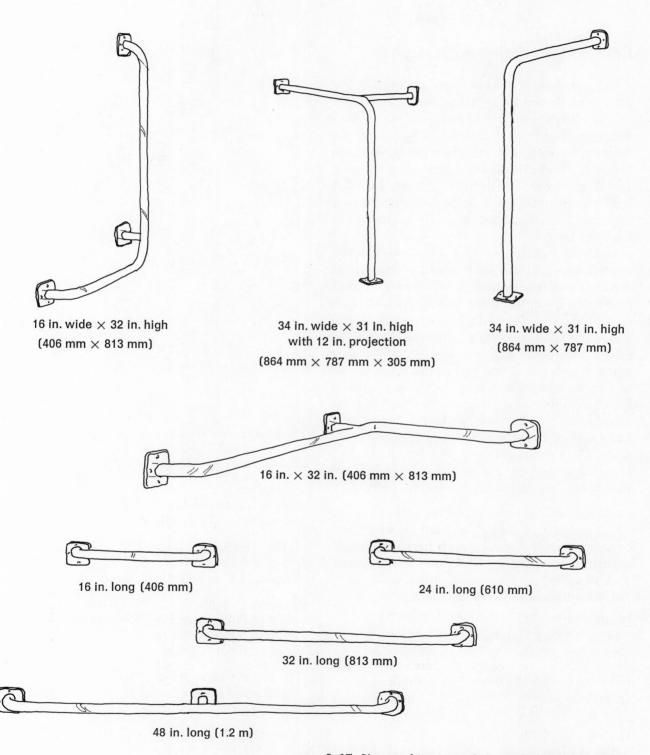

16 in. wide × 32 in. high
(406 mm × 813 mm)

34 in. wide × 31 in. high
with 12 in. projection
(864 mm × 787 mm × 305 mm)

34 in. wide × 31 in. high
(864 mm × 787 mm)

16 in. × 32 in. (406 mm × 813 mm)

16 in. long (406 mm)

24 in. long (610 mm)

32 in. long (813 mm)

48 in. long (1.2 m)

9–17 Size combinations of the Hall Mack 350 Series
of residential and institutional grab bars; you can make
your own combinations.

•

Low-Budget Bathroom Make-over

Typical of bathrooms in many apartments and mass-built homes today is the lineup of fixtures in a small room with a narrow doorway shown in Figure 9–18. First priority is to widen the doorway or keep a small chair on wheels just inside to which the disabled person can transfer. Install grab bars on the door frame. Install a light switch outside the bathroom; use the new silent rocker switch set 36 in./914 mm above the floor level.

Inside the bathroom (see Figure 9–19) you might add a grab bar on the wall at one side of the toilet, or else attach a slip-over guardrail. Replace existing lavatory faucet controls with wristblade handles. Add a narrow shelf just above the faucets. Place a mirror just below the existing medicine cabinet door. Fasten a long vertical grab bar at one end of the tub, and one or two more on the side wall. Place a transfer bench in the tub. Arrange a personal shower attachment within reach of the tub bench, and hang a shower curtain that you've made a slit in to fit (somewhat) over the bench. If floor covering is desired, use smooth, dense low-pile indoor-outdoor carpeting rather than fluffy shag.

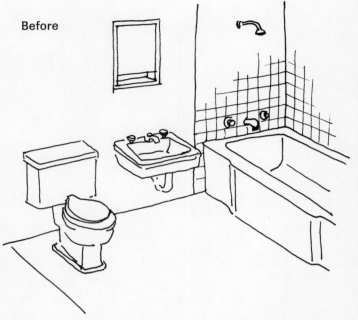

Before

9–18 **Before: small conventional bathroom.**

Mainstream Source List—Bathrooms

American Standard
P.O. Box 2003
New Brunswick, New Jersey 08903

Bradley
Faucet & Special Products Division
Menomonee Falls, Wisconsin 53051

Creative Industries, Inc.
1753 N. Spaulding Avenue
Chicago, Illinois 60647

Hammacher Schlemmer
147 East 57th Street
New York, New York 10022

Johnson Hardware Products, Inc.
P.O. Box 1126
Elkhart, Indiana 46514

MED, Inc.
1215 S. Harlem Avenue
Forest Park, Illinois 60130

Nelson Medical Products
5690 Sarah Avenue
Sarasota, Florida 33581

NuTone–Hall Mack
Housing Products *or* Bath Accessories
Madison & Red Bank Roads
Cincinnati, Ohio 45227

The Braun Corporation
1014 South Monticello
Winamac, Indiana 46996

Whitaker's
230 E. Hartsdale Avenue
Hartsdale, New York 10530

After

9–19 After: small bathroom made safer, more accessible.

Chapter 10

Kitchens —the Better Way

Just the thought of refitting a kitchen for a wheelchaired man or woman causes many families to give up on the whole idea of independent living even before the person is released from the treatment center. Confused about what to do to make a kitchen functional, everyone stops looking for answers. Already weighed down by financial worries, the family balks at adding more expenses to the list. As a result, all plans to continue training and to help the disabled become self-sufficient at home are soon abandoned. Institutional care, after all, seems the only solution.

But there is a better way and it's simply this: ignore the existing kitchen. Forget about trying to uproot and reshape cabinets, ranges, and sinks. Consider instead an Alternate Kitchen: a collection of portable appliances on low, narrow work surfaces arranged in a corner of the existing kitchen or elsewhere in the house or apartment.

An Alternate Kitchen is for relatively temporary situations and is of value for three reasons.

First, it buys some time for you; it gives you a chance to evaluate what the long-term needs are likely to be. Second, it hastens the disabled person's return into the mainstream; he or she can begin to use newly learned rehabilitation techniques without having to wait for a complete kitchen overhaul. And last, an Alternate Kitchen eases financial strain at a time when budgets are already stretched to the limit by medical costs.

Planning an Alternate Kitchen

Since the standard kitchen cabinet and range height is 36 in./914 mm, your first priority will be to set up a new, low work area in some accessible part of the existing kitchen.

Work surfaces in kitchens for the disabled should be 30 to 32 in./762 to 813 mm above floor level, and 16 to 18 in./406 to 457 mm deep (front to back). Also, there should be open space beneath the surfaces so a seated person

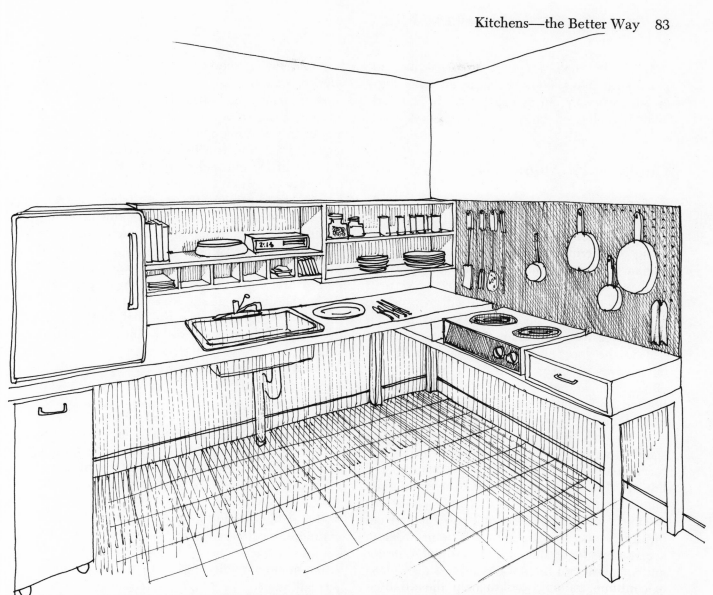

10–1 An Alternate Kitchen set up inside or adjacent to an existing kitchen. Use portable appliances, sturdy narrow tables, and prefinished counter tops.

will have knee room. Therefore, wall-hung shelves, narrow Parsons tables, or planks supported at each end would serve.

The surfaces could be made of butcher block or thick plywood covered in a heat-resistant material such as plastic laminate or ceramic tile.

An L-shaped corner arrangement of shelves or tables is the most efficient to work in because it requires the least amount of turning and mov-

ing on the part of the person working in the kitchen.

A U-shaped setup would be satisfactory, too, provided there is at least 5 ft./1.5 m of space in the middle of the U.

Another possibility is a corridor arrangement —shelves or tables set parallel to each other, 5 ft./1.5 m apart.

The least efficient arrangement is a lineup of everything along one wall; the person would have to do too much moving and turning. But even this would be better than making no changes.

Once you have a new work area planned, place strip plugs along the wall, on table legs, or wherever appliances can be safely and conveniently plugged in.

Outfitting an Alternate Kitchen

Meals can be prepared with a few of the many portable appliances on the market. For instance, an electric skillet, tabletop broiler oven, toaster oven, or microwave oven can substitute for a standard range or built-in oven. (Ranges and wall ovens should be disconnected.) A small two-burner hotplate can be used for surface cooking. An automatic coffee maker would be a safe source for small amounts of hot water.

Take the doors off the base cabinets, add roll-out shelves or Lazy Susans, and use these for china, linen, and glassware as well as for canned, bottled, and packaged goods. Store infrequently used items in the wall cabinets above.

Hang pots, pans, and lids on straight, up-slanted pegs mounted on the wall at a comfortable level. Don't use hooks; pan handles and lids are difficult to lift up and over the curved ends of hooks.

Take the doors off the sink cabinet and cut out all or part of the cabinet floor in order to create some leg space under the sink. Drainpipe and sink will still be in the way, but the person can manage to get a little closer, nevertheless. Cover or wrap the pipes so that legs don't get burned.

The strain of reaching down into a deep sink set in a too-high counter can be eased by placing a plastic dish drainer face down in the bottom of the sink. Cook pots and dishpan can rest on this. Automatic dishwashers are excellent time- and strength-savers for the disabled; have one if space and budget permit.

Replace two-handle faucet controls with a new single-lever unit if you can. Otherwise bring existing faucet controls within easy reach by fastening long wooden handles to the controls with wire, metal strips, rubber bands, or waterproof tape.

There's not much you need do to make an existing refrigerator accessible, since the shelves are already low enough to reach. But the problem of defrosting is a big one for the disabled because lifting out and carrying a thin, shallow drip tray of water from refrigerator to sink is a drenching business. Perhaps a friend or relative can volunteer to take care of this chore at regular intervals. Manufacturers might note that the nondisabled would be most grateful for a neater way to dispose of defrost water, too. One enterprising homemaker (nondisabled) punched drain holes in the plastic tray with a heated ice pick and set a dishpan on the shelf below. The deep pan is much easier to lift and carry to the sink.

Frost-free refrigerators are another excellent appliance for the disabled; have one if space and budget permit.

Except for the slight damage done to the floor of the sink cabinet, you've made a workable kitchen inside a standard one with a minimum of effort and money. Even a rented house or apartment could be outfitted with an Alternate Kitchen.

But if the existing kitchen is inaccessible, or unsuitable for some reason, an Alternate can be set up elsewhere. In Figure 10–1, for example, is what one might call a flip-flop kitchen, set up in a small 6 × 9 ft./1.8 × 2.7 m dining area at the end of an original kitchen—which, by the way, is left intact. A first-floor powder room on the other side of the end wall would simplify plumbing connections. This Alternate Kitchen could be arranged in a private house for a disabled person who did not want to give up his or her home or independence. An Alternate Kitchen right next to the permanent one can be dismantled at some future time and will not affect the resale value of the house.

A shallow stainless steel sink, fitted with a single-lever faucet, is centered in a 9 ft./2.7 m plastic laminated counter top braced along the

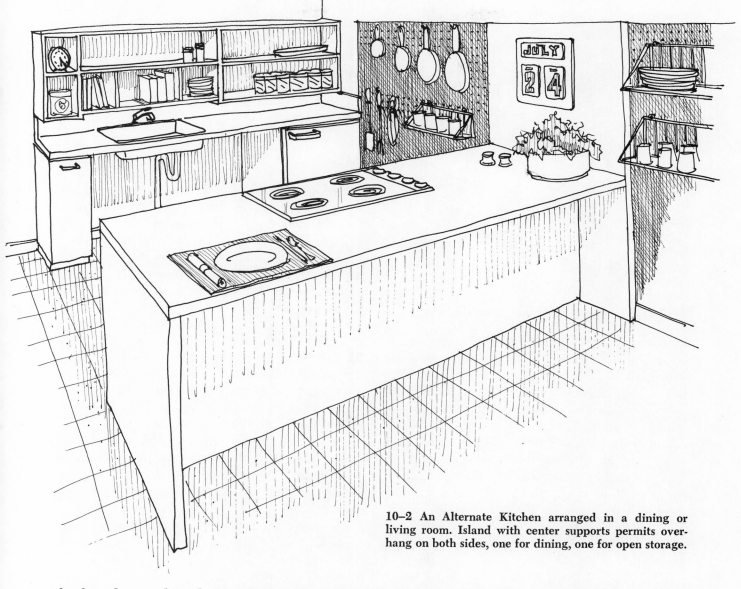

10–2 An Alternate Kitchen arranged in a dining or living room. Island with center supports permits overhang on both sides, one for dining, one for open storage.

back and at each end. A compact counter-top refrigerator holds supplies transferred as needed from the larger one in the original kitchen, nearby. Underneath the counter is a roll-out pantry (see Figure 10–3) for canned and packaged provisions. Open shelves above the sink hold china, glassware, and other necessities within reach. A 6 ft./1.8 m Parsons table was cut down to slide under sink counter to form a workable L-shape. It holds a two-burner portable range wedged between the counter and a small one-drawer unit of equal height so that hot or heavy pots can be pushed to and from the range rather than lifted. Pans and cooking utensils hang on the wall behind the table. A microwave oven on a rolling cart would complete the Alternate Kitchen. The surface of the sink counter is 32 in./813 mm above floor level; that of the table is 27 in./686 mm above the floor.

Tiny kitchens in many apartments are totally

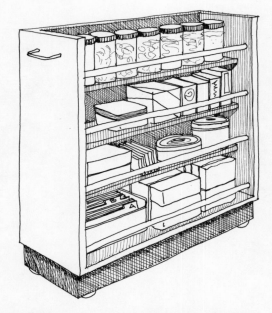

10–3 Roll-out pantry; make it of plywood or pine.

inaccessible, but an Alternate Kitchen can be set up in one end of a large room, as has been done in Figure 10–2. Try to place it in a room that backs onto existing plumbing. The white Formica room divider–cooktop counter is as long as space will allow, 32 in./813 mm high and 48 in./1.2 m wide. A full-length center support provides a 24 in./610 mm overhang for dining on one side and space for kitchen storage, including a portable oven, on the other. A stainless steel sink with an off-center drain (see Figure 10–4) is flanked by an under-counter refrigerator on the right and a roll-out pantry on the left. Open shelves, lined in navy blue, and navy blue pegboard panels hold kitchen and dining utensils. Ceiling-mounted track lighting provides illumination for kitchen and contains down-lighting spots for dining.

The roll-out pantry in Figure 10–3, a feature of most kitchens planned by the Institute of Rehabilitation Medicine home-planning consultant, is a simple free-standing shallow storage unit that can be pulled into position anywhere in the room. It is not sold commercially, so it has to be custom-made or homemade. If you

think of it as a shallow drawer set on edge and mounted on a low platform fitted with large ball casters, you have the basic idea. Add shelves with little guardrails and a D-shaped pull handle, and the unit is complete. Keep it narrow so the contents are always within view and easy reach.

An Endless Search

Seek-and-find is a cruel game the disabled and their families are forced to play as they try to turn their dream of independent living into reality. They must search through the millions of household products sold by thousands of merchants and wholesalers to find the handful of fixtures, furnishings, and appliances the disabled can use. Clues to products and sources turn into false leads; frustrations build.

To their credit, the disabled can make do with almost anything, and the nondisabled find they can modify all kinds of shapes and objects once they catch on to what's needed and why.

In recent years some industries have begun to study the problem of supplying the disabled with suitable goods and services. But all too frequently these manufacturers are proceeding on the mistaken premise that two separate groups of products have to be made—one for the disabled and one for the nondisabled—and that two design-sales-and-marketing systems have to be created as well. Yet more often than not, manufacturers already have disability-oriented products and don't know it. They are not aware of it simply because various products come into being as a result of new technologies, changes in consumer demand, or a specialized need in segments of their own industry. A telling example of this is the 5½-in.-deep kitchen sink, which wasn't developed for the disabled but happens to be an answer to one of their prayers.

Standard kitchen sinks are about 7 in. deep, not a comfortable depth for someone who must prepare meals and wash dishes from a seated position. The disabled could spend untold hours looking in obscure places for a more shallow sink. Then, a few years ago, kitchen dealers began showing a dishwasher-under-the-sink combination which just happened to require a shallow sink only 5½ in. deep (see Figure 10–4). Not only that, there had to be a side drain rather than a center one because of the dishwasher below. For the disabled, nothing could have been better: less depth and no center drain to bump against. What's more, the sink can be bought separately, is made by Elkay, a nationally known maker, and is available at kitchen dealers and plumbing supply stores (Model No. GECR-2521, with choice of right or left side drain).

Single-lever control faucets (sold separately and not part of the above-mentioned sink) are another blessing that came along on the wings of new product development. While not designed for the disabled per se, they couldn't have been better done if they had been. They are widely available for under $35.

None of the products in Figures 10–5 to 10–15 was designed especially for the disabled, but each has features that can suit particular needs. These are but a few of the thousands of items you'll find in stores and catalogues as you shop for something special. Keep in mind what the person can and cannot do, and judge an item or appliance accordingly: Are knobs and buttons large or small? do doors swing up, down, right, or left? can it tip over easily? is it too light, too heavy? can it be operated with one hand? does it require two hands? etc.

Special note: for the visually impaired, the General Electric Company will provide Braille knobs for its ranges free of charge. If you know someone with this disability who has a General Electric range, you can request the special knobs by sending the model number of the range to Jim Buxton, General Electric Company, Building 2-210, Appliance Park, Louisville, Kentucky 40225.

General Electric and Hotpoint appliance use and care manuals are available on tape for the visually impaired. Tapes can be ordered from the Center for Consumer Products Recording, P.O. Box 306, Louisville, Kentucky 40201. Indicate product, brand, model number, and year purchased, if known. Include $1.25 to cover cost of cassette and packaging for the mails.

The Permanent Kitchen

Whether building from scratch or remodeling, a permanent kitchen for wheelchair cooks will

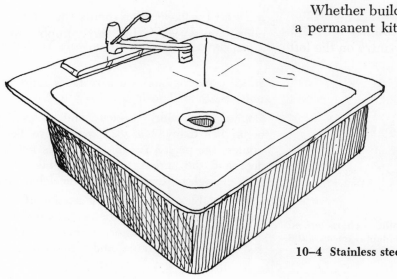

10–4 Stainless steel sink, 5½ in./140 mm deep; Elkay.

10–5 Substitutions for conventional ranges and ovens:

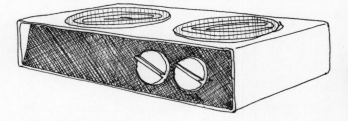

A. **Portable table-top range. Look for front controls, big easy-to-turn knobs or dials. Widely available for under $30.**

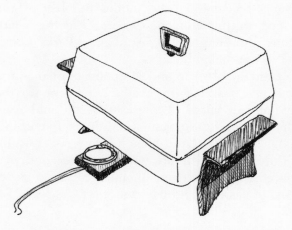

B. **Electric skillet. Should have control that is detachable, and have a sturdy base. Sold everywhere for $25 and up.**

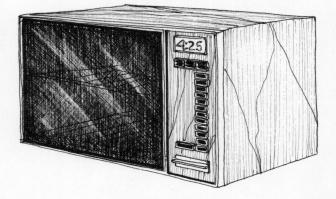

C. **Microwave oven. Ideal for disabilities characterized by weakness, and those prone to accidental burns. $200 to $500.**

D. **Toaster oven. Look for easy-to-handle controls and flip-up door. Widely available for from $23 up to about $60.**

E. **Counter-top range. Must have on-off switch, large door handle, and firmly hinged door. From $50 to about $150.**

have all the basic ingredients that standard kitchens have except for three important differences:

Sinks, cooktops, and work surfaces must be open underneath to allow leg room.

Counter tops, work surfaces, and tables shouldn't be higher than 32 in./813 mm above floor level (unless the person is tall); the space between the floor and the underside of the surface should be high enough to accommodate wheelchair armrests.

Shelves, tables, and work surfaces should be narrow enough to accommodate the person's reach: 8 to 10 in./203 to 254 mm for storage shelves; 16 to 18 in./406 to 457 mm for tables and counter tops.

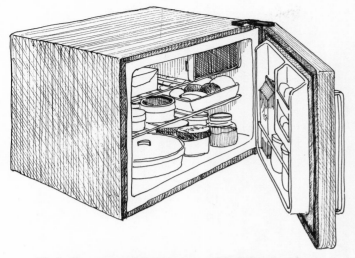

10–6 Compact refrigerators are ideal for an Alternate Kitchen. Set on counter or under it, whichever is best for person's reach. Available at kitchen dealers, JC Penney, Sears, Berg & Brown.

10–7 Small gas and electric cooktops solve space and budget problems.

A. Gas cooktop. Look for front controls with large knobs. At local kitchen dealers or can be ordered from Berg & Brown or W & L Manufacturing Company.

B. Two-burner electric cooktop. Also at local kitchen dealers or can be ordered from Berg & Brown or W & L Manufacturing Company.

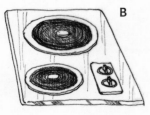

If, by this, you think the whole kitchen will have to be expensively custom-made, be reassured. There really are furnishings and cabinetry, in the styles and colors you prefer, that are ready-made and waiting to be fitted together any way you want. All kinds of equipment and appliances have been created to serve the new trends toward flexible kitchen design—and the disabled benefit from it.

For instance, there are double-bowl sinks that have one bowl shallower than the other. With the sink set into an open counter, a seated person can fit comfortably under the shallow-bowl part of the sink. American Standard, for one, makes

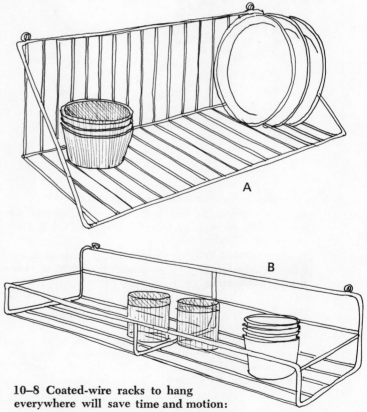

10–8 Coated-wire racks to hang everywhere will save time and motion:

A. Handy dish drainer for drying and storing china, glassware, or for keeping things in easy reach. From Seabon for about $10.

B. Small hanging shelf for cans, utensils, whatever. From Seabon for $3. For these and many more racks and baskets, write for catalogue.

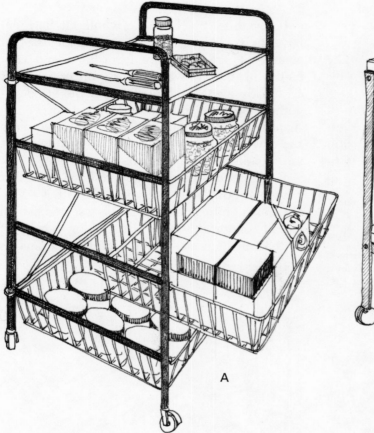

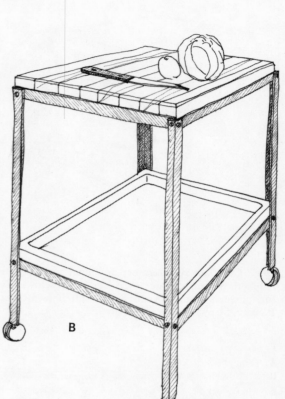

A

B

10–9 Let rolling carts and tables lift and carry.

A. Three roomy baskets and top tray slide out for accessibility to supplies of all kinds. About $30 from Hammacher Schlemmer.

B. Cutting-block table is sturdy enough to hold microwave or tabletop oven. Approximately $40 from Hammacher Schlemmer.

10–10 A food processor will slice, grind, mix, grate, shred, mince, or blend in seconds. Safety interlock prevents accidental motor start-up. Good finger coordination necessary. By General Electric for about $90.

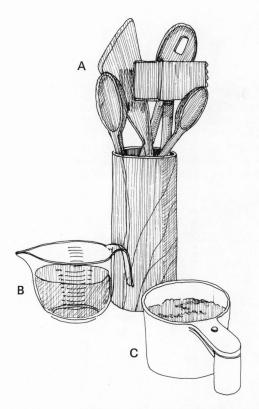

10–12 More utensils that are easy to handle:

A. Thick, smooth solid plastic kitchenware that is pleasant to hold; won't come apart if dropped. At many housewares stores.

B. Totally contemporary: deep, straight-sided plates and saucers. Perfect for many disabled to eat from; unbreakable. Affordable, too.

C. Matching mugs with wide **D**-shaped handles add up to more convenience. A Heller Design widely available in import and housewares shops.

D. Bold, new stainless steel flatware with big bamboo and plastic handles that are easy to grip. The disabled appreciate this trend!

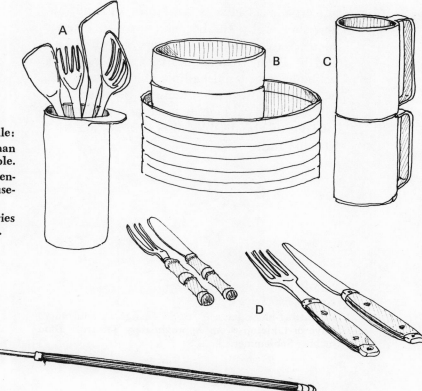

10–11 Some utensils that are especially easy to handle:

A. Wooden kitchen implements are easier to grip than thin metal ones, feel comfortable too. Widely available.

B. Clear Lucite mix-and-measure bowl has wide open-end handle and skid-resistant base. At better housewares shops for $5.

C. Thick-handled cordless electric flour sifter; batteries are included. From Hammacher Schlemmer for $11.

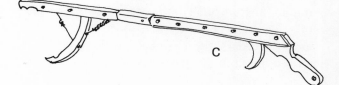

10–13 Only one of these quick helpers was designed for the disabled:

A. Telescopic feather duster on an aluminum rod; washable plumes. Extends to 6 ft./1.8 m. At Hammacher Schlemmer for $15.

B. Double-tong grab-all 30 in./762 mm extension gripper for reaching high places. From Hammacher Schlemmer for $8.

C. Folding extension gripper is a mere 6 oz./170 g; extends 22 in./559 mm and folds to 12½ in./318 mm. From Maddak, Inc., for $20.

a kitchen sink of this kind—the Fiesta No. 7130.040—with one bowl 4½ in./114 mm deep.

Single-lever faucets, already mentioned, can be mounted at the right or left of the sink. Where is it written that faucets must always be at the back?

Wall cabinets, 30 in./762 mm high, in any color or finish you might desire, when set on a low recessed base or short legs, can serve as base cabinets when outfitted with tops of butcher block, solid maple slabs, or plywood covered in one of the heat-resistant plastic laminates. Storage organizers such as turntables, slide-out bins, and shelves by Rubbermaid provide "drawer" space. See local kitchen dealers as well as Sears and JC Penney catalogues for ready-made wall cabinets and prefinished counter tops.

There is now a manufacturer making 32 in./813 mm base cabinets with large toe-space specifically for the disabled. For information, write Merillat Industries, Inc.

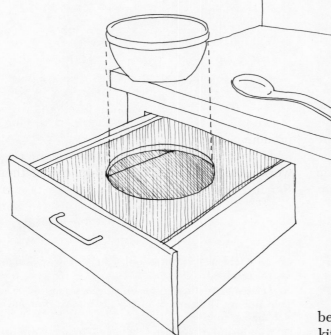

10–14 An ordinary drawer becomes a pull-out mixing center. It's not sold anywhere but you can make one to fit any drawer. Use pine or plywood; sand well and cut hole for bowl to sit in.

10–15 Everyone should practice fire safety at home. A. Norelco fire extinguisher under an attractive cover. For grease, gasoline, paint, electrical fires. At department, housewares stores. B. General Electric Home Sentry smoke alarm. Have either a battery-powered, plug-in, or direct-wire model. At hardware and housewares stores.

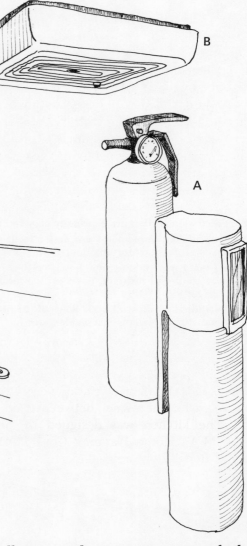

Wall ovens and microwave ovens, which can be mounted at any convenient height, add to kitchen flexibility. The many cooktop surface units for counter tops, such as those by Thermador, Tappan, Whirlpool, Caloric, and others, increase flexibility even more.

Range hoods are now ductless and can be installed anywhere, at any height.

Frost-free refrigerators, automatic dishwashers, trash compactors, washers and dryers, instant-hot-water sink attachments, garbage disposers: all these make independent living more attainable.

The city apartment kitchen in Figure 10–16 was remodeled for the owner-occupant, who was disabled in a skiing accident. The original wall cabinets, dishwasher, refrigerator, and range with eye-level ovens remain unchanged. The standard sink and its base cabinets were replaced by a lowered sink with open space and roll-out supply cart (see Figure 10–3) beneath it. The owner was lucky enough to have a shallow range with burners in a single row. (This range model has since been discontinued.) Storage space and doors below the cooking surface were removed to permit a closer approach to the range. In the space between the new, lowered sink and the original wall cabinets is a shallow 8 in./203 mm storage unit for holding supplies within convenient reach. Think of it as a wall-hung bookcase fitted with vertical dividers.

To get turn-around space for the wheelchair, the base cabinets on the left wall were replaced by an L-shaped wall-hung shelf (see Figure 10–16A). This shelf narrows at one end to allow ample room for the owner between it and the range. The kitchen was designed by Sharon Wright, M.A., Home Planning Consultant, Institute of Rehabilitation Medicine, N.Y.U. Medical Center. The contractor: Berg & Brown, Inc., New York, New York.

Two permanent kitchens in private homes, one in Pennsylvania, the other in California, contain only standard sinks, ranges, and the like because their owners are tall and have long arms. However, both owners did make modifications which they feel will not affect the resale value of the houses. In both kitchens, the space beneath the sink and cooktop surface units has been left open for closer wheelchair

approach. One homeowner uses a wall oven and finds it comfortable. The other, who has multiple sclerosis, has no conventional oven in the kitchen, preferring to use instead a microwave or portable oven, both of which are kept on a rolling cart.

Connecticut homeowners Jim and Dorothy L. have a kitchen that is so large they were able to keep the original intact and build another complete one inside it. It features a long cooktop–snack counter at right angles to one wall. Narrow wall-hung storage cabinets flank both sides; a stainless steel double sink has one shallow bowl that allows accessibility to the sink counter, the frost-free refrigerator has slide-out shelves, and there's an automatic dishwasher. According to the L.'s, the resilient vinyl floor of simulated brick needs very little care. All work surfaces are 28 in./711 mm above floor level. The vent above the cooktop is operated by a switch fastened to the underside of the counter.

Tips from Wheelchair Cooks

Use inexpensive, very lightweight pots, pans, and dishtowels if lifting and holding things is difficult. Use heavy pots and pans if tremor is pronounced and frequent.

Arrange utensils and appliances close to all work areas, even if it means duplicating them. For instance, Dorothy L. has supplies of paper towels and food wraps in four different locations. She also keeps long barbecue tongs hanging in various places in every room in the house to retrieve things that fall or are too high to reach.

Unbreakable plastic containers and stainless steel bowls are a must.

Use roll-out racks, bins, baskets, shelf trays, and Lazy Susans everywhere you can.

Of course, there are hundreds more ideas and good advice that would take many pages to list. There are two excellent booklets filled with invaluable tips. One *The Wheelchair in the*

10–16 A city apartment kitchen, modified for a wheel-chaired homemaker. New, lower sink was only major change. Wall-hung shelf on left wall replaces a cumbersome base cabinet, allows more floor space, close-approach work surface. Wall cabinets, appliances were unchanged. Floor plan (A) remains the same, though kitchen is now accessible.

stitute of Rehabilitation Medicine, N.Y.U. Medical Center, and the Campbell Soup Company. It costs $3.25, including postage, and can be ordered from Mealtime Manual, Box 38, Ronks, Pennsylvania 17572.

Kitchen, which costs $2.50. Send check or money order to Kitchens, Paralyzed Veterans of America, Inc., 7315 Wisconsin Avenue N.W., Washington, D.C. 20014.

The other is *Mealtime Manual for People with Disabilities and the Aging,* prepared by the In-

Mainstream Source List—Kitchens

American Standard
P.O. Box 2003
New Brunswick, New Jersey 08903

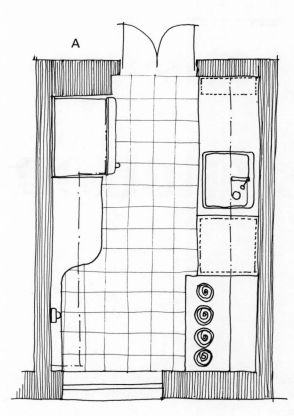

A

Hammacher Schlemmer
147 East 57 Street
New York, New York 10022

JC Penney
Local stores and catalogue
Maddack, Inc.
Pequannock, New Jersey 07440

Merillat Industries, Inc.
2075 West Beecher Road
Adrian, Michigan 49221

Rubbermaid Corporation
Wooster, Ohio 44692

Seabon Scandinavian Imports
54 East 54th Street
New York, New York 10022

Sears
Local stores and catalogue

Tappan Appliance Group
Tappan Park
Mansfield, Ohio 44901

Berg & Brown, Inc.
1424 Lexington Avenue
New York, New York 10028

Thermador
5119 District Boulevard
Los Angeles, California 90022

Caloric Corporation
Topton, Pennsylvania 19562

W & L Manufacturing Co., Inc.
343 Cortlandt Street
Belleville, New Jersey 07109

Elkay Manufacturing Company
2700 S. 17th Avenue
Broadview, Illinois 60153

Whirlpool Corporation
Benton Harbor, Michigan 49022

Chapter 11

New Construction

At this point, you are more knowledgeable about many details of building and remodeling for the disabled than most contractors—not, however, because the preceding chapters are a complete course in home construction, nor because professional builders refuse to know or care. You are qualified because you know why things need to be done a certain way, and you know what the disabled person can and cannot do in terms of taking care of himself or herself at home.

Your understanding of the whys, and your patient explanation of them, will be one of the most important contributions you can make in dealings with architects and contractors on behalf of the disabled.

For instance, if a builder understands that the person must transfer from wheelchair to toilet from a side position, right or left, and that three or four feet of clear space at the side of the fixture is needed for the transfer, and that the seat must be on the same level as the wheelchair seat, he will know how to lay out the room and to order fixturing.

Similarly, it won't be enough to tell him that the shower or tub controls must be placed at a convenient height in the side wall rather than in the end wall; he will have to know how far above the floor they must be and where on the side wall to place them. No builder can know how far the person can reach or if one arm is stronger than the other unless you tell him.

Shopping for and getting a builder interested in taking the job will be less time-consuming and frustrating for you if you go to him with a list of as many sizes and locations of features as you can possibly provide. What's more, if you can supply the brand name, model number, or source of certain products—a shallow sink, for example, or a lavatory with a side drain—you've made the job easier for him, his subcontractors, and yourself.

Home builders and remodelers tend to think of creating structures for the disabled, whether one room or a whole house, as a highly specialized operation involving miles of red tape. They envision having to order institutional products from suppliers they don't regularly do business with. In short order, though, you should be able to convince a builder that this is not the case; that very few if any doors, light switches, equipment, fixtures, or materials need be different from those he is accustomed to handling. They will only be planned for with more care than usual, and placed at levels that are different from those he generally uses. But if you can supply him with the details that help make a room addition or a house functional for a disabled child or adult, he will have fewer qualms about taking the assignment.

Moreover, if you can act as a diplomatic on-site observer, or liaison, if you will, between the contractor and the various jobbers he assigns to the project, the construction process might go along more smoothly. For while the builder may understand why a room or house has to have certain features, or be done a particular way, the subcontractors may not have gotten the message as clearly.

One astute homeowner who had contracted for some extensive house remodeling—an adult family member had recently become disabled—anticipated this possibility. He handled it in a way that pleased the contractor and caused no friction between himself and the workmen.

All he did was keep an old wheelchair near the building site. Whenever a question or some confusion arose about placement or whatever, he'd pull up the chair and sit in it to determine whether one solution would be more sensible than another for the disabled person. He never suggested that any of the men follow his example, but they invariably did whenever they wanted to get a better fix on how to arrange spaces and fixtures for someone in a seated position.

It must be pointed out that if this remodeling project had been done for a disabled child, the workman-in-the-wheelchair technique would not have been satisfactory since the dimensions within which a child can operate are different than those for adults. Where children are concerned, be guided by what the child can do:

determine by actual measurement how far he can reach, bend, and turn. Have the child's doctor or nurse help you get this information, and have it with you when you consult builders or architects.

Finding the Way

Professional builders are aware of the many rules and specifications that can be involved in building for the disabled. They also know that many of these regulations are vague and subject to unending interpretation. Furthermore, all building guidelines so far developed for the disabled pertain to public buildings and housing. There are no guidelines for private residences and their owners. All the more reason why you, and the disabled to the extent possible, will have to lead, guide, and suggest the best way to build.

It may seem like an unwieldy alliance, but in this instance the private contractor will welcome all the help you can offer. There's little else to rely on but yourselves.

A family living in a Midwest farming community found this out four years ago. They wanted to build a room addition onto their home for their disabled son. The boy had been injured in an auto accident the year before and now, wheelchaired but active, needed a room of his own.

The parents' plea for information about building and equipping a room and bath for a disabled youngster resulted in their being sent a four-page photostated copy of specifications for building public and commercial structures. Very little of it was helpful and all of it was frustrating to them.

Appeals to official agencies and other organizations for sources of products or building tips netted them off-the-point answers and referrals to persons or groups who in turn referred them to other persons and groups.

One request for ramp-building instructions, offered free by a disability-interest group, got them a form letter stating that the response was greater than expected and as soon as a new batch of instructions was printed, they would receive their copy. They are still waiting.

After more frustrations of this kind, the family realized it was up to them. They planned the room, figured out dimensions as best they could, and, working with several contractors as needed, got the room addition completed. They say they made a few mistakes—a doorway could have been better placed—but all in all, the room is functional and pleasant.

Another family, in Pennsylvania, also experienced an infuriating round of unfulfilled promises, false leads, and vague answers to specific questions. They finally decided to go it on their own. With the help of friends and contractors whom they called in as needed, they succeeded in building an attractive ground-floor wing onto their Colonial-styled home for their ten-year-old daughter, Betsy. Though she spends most of her time in a wheelchair, Betsy is an active, outgoing youngster who gets around at times with crutches and braces and leads an active life among family and school friends.

Since Betsy's mother and father realized other parents would be up against the same barriers they encountered, they allowed the new wing to be photographed to appear in a national magazine article.* They also gave permission to have a detailed floor plan of the room made available to the public through the National Easter Seal Society. (For ordering a copy of *A Special Child's Room*, see Mainstream Source List at the end of this chapter.)

Betsy's Room

Betsy's parents designed a spacious (17 ft. long by 15 ft. 4 in. wide/5.2 m by 4.8 m) wing which they divided into three general areas inside: a bath with roll-in shower, a closet–dressing room, and a bedroom-study-playroom measuring about

* *1,001 Decorating Ideas,* March/April 1976.

9 by 17 ft./2.7 by 5.2 m. The entire floor is covered in smooth, firm indoor-outdoor carpeting, and the color scheme is Betsy's own: bright yellow, green, and white.

The bedroom-study-playroom is pictured in Figure 11–1. The platform bed is level with the wheelchair seat and is near enough to the wall shelves for Betsy to reach books, radio, and games. The top shelf is 38 in./965 mm above floor level and the shelves are 10 in./245 mm deep (front to back). Window sills are 20 in./508 mm above the floor; window shades are fitted with long cords which pass through a pulley latch mounted on each sill. (See Figure 5–9, page 38, for close-up.) Light switches and outlets are easy for Betsy to reach while seated. The doorways—there are only two—are 36 in./914 mm wide. Furniture and accessories are functional yet fun (all came from JC Penney), and there's nothing in the room, such as frills or gimmicks, to obstruct or frustrate her in moving about and caring for herself. (For a close-up of the dressing room with closet, see Figure 7–3, page 54.)

The 6 by 9 ft./1.8 by 2.7 m bathroom (see Figure 11–2) contains a counter-top lavatory that's 31 in./787 mm high and just wide enough to safely support the oval sink with single-lever faucet. A set of plastic drawers is hung on the underside of the counter top on the left, and on the right is a roll-out storage unit with pivoting shallow trays (actually a cabinet for artists found in an art-supply store). A window, centered in the lavatory alcove, provides natural light; mirrors are on the side walls, and there's a recessed light in the soffit above. Safety handrails surround the toilet. Except for the shower stall itself, this room is fully carpeted.

In her shower chair (see Figure 11–2), Betsy can bathe unassisted. The entry to the shower is floor-level and carpeted; the shower floor slopes gently downward toward the center drain.

The shower compartment itself (see Figure 11–3) is 3 ft./914 mm square, ceramic-tiled,

11–1 View of room addition built by Betsy's parents. Room design by Michael Kennedy for JC Penney Co.

11–2 Spaces, fixtures, and built-ins are arranged in ways that make this bathroom accessible to young person seated in wheeled shower chair.

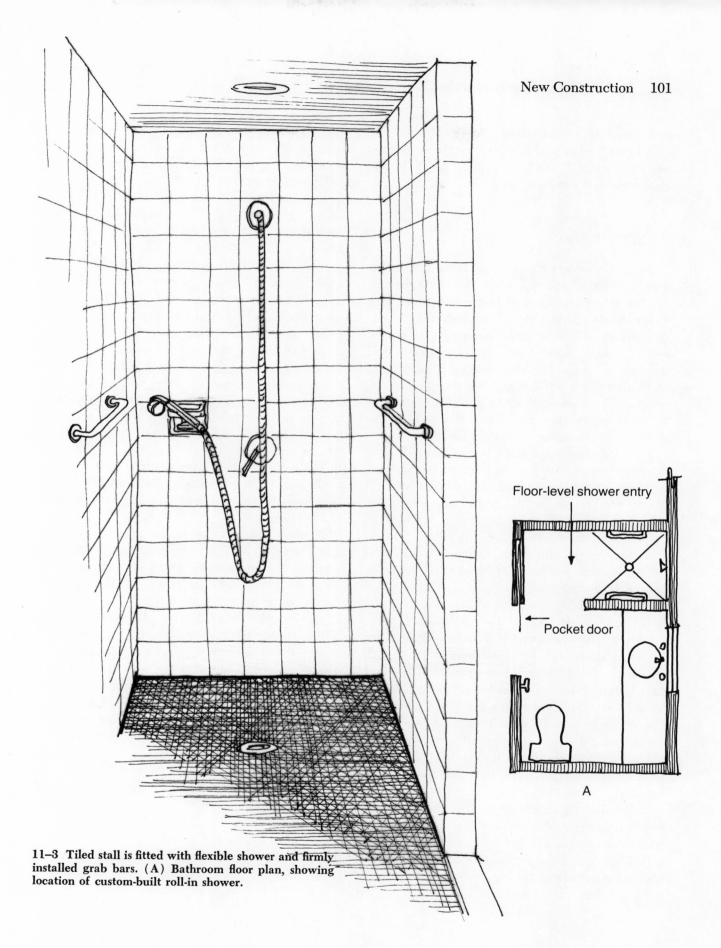

Floor-level shower entry

Pocket door

A

11–3 Tiled stall is fitted with flexible shower and firmly installed grab bars. (A) Bathroom floor plan, showing location of custom-built roll-in shower.

and fitted with grab bars. A flexible shower attachment with a single-lever water-and-temperature control handle is set 28 in./711 mm above the shower-floor level.

A New House

Betty G., owner of this one-level California home, worked closely with the builder-contractor to get the kind of house she wanted: a spacious contemporary with Spanish nuances expressed in subtle exterior archways, textured roofing, and rich contrasts of stucco and weathered wood. She also wanted a swimming pool. Betty is a post-polio who, though she depends upon a wheelchair to get around, drives to work every day and looks forward to her daily swim when she returns home.

In discussing her house, Betty says, "It is a must for an architect or builder to become familiar with the individual needs of a disabled client. He has to get to know the person for whom the house is being built. He can look at similar houses and read the official guidelines, but there is no one place he can find all the variations that are going to be needed by every prospective customer.

"The first thing to do," she says, "is to get the builder, and his wife if she works with him, interested in your individual needs. My builder was recommended by the friend of a friend. We discussed the number of rooms and the fact that I wanted a pool, then looked at the budget to see what could be done. He and I designed the room layout. I knew I wanted a Spanish design, and he had some great ideas. He also helped me find the lot. I had previously talked to several other builders, but they weren't interested.

"Our close association during the planning phase paid off and I had no problem getting a well-designed, functional house with all the details I wanted. I did learn later that the builder spotted some errors during construction but he had them corrected right away. One mistake, for example, concerned the central vacuum system I had requested. The outlets were supposed to be placed so that I could reach them easily. But the workmen were installing them in the usual places, on the baseboard. My builder caught the error and had it corrected before I knew anything about it.

"This illustrates how really dependent upon a builder the disabled person is. I would not have been able to check out the project as it progressed, but he could and did."

The floor plan of Betty G.'s house is shown in Figure 11–4. Extra interior space was gained by designing the house to angle outward toward the property line on one side. Sliding windows are used throughout. The floor-level patio and sunken pool are in view of, and accessible from, both the master bedroom wing and the living-dining area.

The entry porch is a gentle, wall-to-wall ramp with a one-in-twelve slope (the step is 3 in./76 mm high, therefore the ramp extends outward 3 ft./914 mm).

Inside, beyond the wide Spanish door (42 in./ 1,067 mm) is an entry with skylight above. At left are the guest bath and bedroom and the master suite, which can be closed off by pocket doors for extra privacy.

Beyond the entry and to the right are the living room, with raised-hearth fireplace, the study, the dining room, and the kitchen, with a pocket door at one end and a ramped (1/12) doorway into the garage at the other.

Because Betty G. is tall and has long arms, she chose standard 36 in./914 mm high cabinets for the kitchen, although the cooktop counter is 32 in./813 mm above the floor and is open underneath, as is the sink, to permit closer approach for the wheelchair. A dishwasher with roll-out racks is a must, she feels, and an automatic washer and a dryer in the kitchen are two conveniences she wouldn't do without. The laundry equipment has front controls and is front-loading. Counter tops are covered in

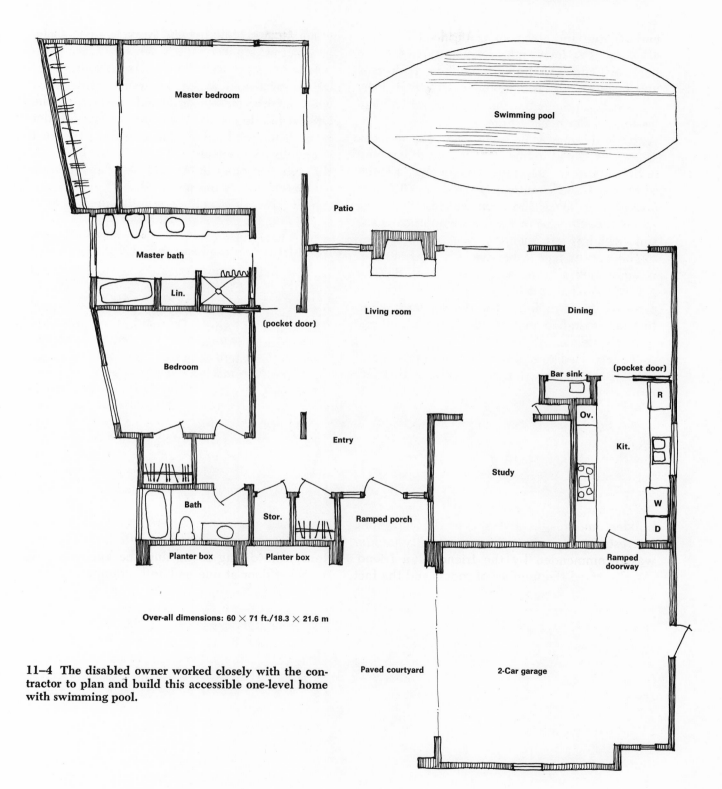

Master bedroom

Swimming pool

Patio

Master bath

Lin.

(pocket door)

Living room

Dining

Bedroom

(pocket door)

Bar sink

R

Ov.

Kit.

Entry

Study

W

D

Bath

Stor.

Ramped porch

Ramped doorway

Planter box

Planter box

Over-all dimensions: 60 × 71 ft./18.3 × 21.6 m

11–4 The disabled owner worked closely with the contractor to plan and build this accessible one-level home with swimming pool.

Paved courtyard

2-Car garage

ceramic tile and the floor is surfaced in vinyl.

Dense, low-level pile carpeting covers the floors in living and dining room, both bedrooms and master bath. Tongue-in-groove wood flooring is used in the entry, guest bath, and hallway leading to the master suite.

Inside the master bedroom wing are an oversized closet and bathroom. Bidet, toilet, and bathtub are all standard in size and height. Vanity sink and counter top are 32 in./813 mm above floor level and have enclosed storage space beneath, except for the section below the sink, which is left open.

The shower had to be specially made to permit easy access. It measures 3½ by 5 ft./1.66 by 1.5 m, and has a padded built-in seat that is 17½ in./444 mm above the shower floor. Grab bars are installed in both the shower and the bathtub alcove.

"I have tried to use standard equipment and fixtures throughout, not only because they are easier to find, but for the resale value of the house, too."

Betty G.'s advice is clear. Get to know your builder and help him to know and understand what the disabled person's needs are likely to be. Official building guidelines are useful—up to a point. They can help set the stage but they don't complete the setting. That has to be done through communication and self-discovery on the part of everyone involved.

Mainstream Source List—New Construction

For a copy of *A Special Child's Room*, send one dollar ($1) in check or money order payable to the National Easter Seal Society for Crippled Children and Adults. Send to: Publications, National Easter Seal Society, 2023 West Ogden Avenue, Chicago, Illinois 60612. All proceeds go to the National Easter Seal campaign.

Chapter 12

Mainstreaming –What It Is

If you paddle a canoe long enough through creeks, branches, and tributaries, you will reach a mainstream, or principal watercourse, from which you will be able to touch, see, smell, and feel all that nature intended you to experience.

To educators, mainstreaming means bringing all children, the disabled and nondisabled, together in buildings and classrooms that are accessible to everyone, so that no child is segregated or treated in any special way because of a physical impairment.

However you choose to interpret it, mainstreaming, to the disabled, is an active word meaning moving along with the majority of the population and having access to the goods and services available to this greater number.

Wanting to be where the action is is not the same as the desire to climb the mountain simply because it's there. The reason is deeper than that, although it is no different from the one that urges the nondisabled onward each day: to have dignity, freedom from want and fear, the right to make decisions—in a word, independence.

Specialists in rehabilitation medicine for some time now have been responding to these inner drives with wonder. The success of their and their patients' efforts inspires new research which in turn produces new wonders.

Caught up in this magnificent cycle, these professionals can see better than most the tremendous potential of these men, women, and children, as well as the problems they will face. Perhaps their admiration and anxiety are best expressed by Dr. Howard A. Rusk in his description of the satisfactions he gains from working with the disabled and his concern for them as they fight their way into the mainstream.

"You don't get fine china by putting clay in the sun. You have to put the clay through the white heat of the kiln if you want to make porcelain. Heat breaks some pieces. Life breaks some people. Disability breaks some people. But once the clay goes through the white-hot fire and comes out whole, it can never be clay again; once a person overcomes a disability through his own courage, determination and hard work, he has a depth of spirit you and I know little about.

"I've now been around such people in great numbers for almost thirty years. I never get tired of them, never stop learning from them, perhaps because after all this time I know that I still have so much to learn from them. Rehabilitation is one branch of medicine in which the patient has more power than the doctor in setting the limits and possibilities. The doctor can tell the patient what to do, but only the patient himself can decide how much he's going to do. In making these decisions, patients are constantly teaching us doctors new things about rehabilitation by proving that they can do more than we had presumed possible.

"Thanks to such patients and to a growing number of dedicated doctors, as well as a select group of financially generous people and many understanding, dedicated public servants, the concept and practice of rehabilitation have made a good start in the world. But while public acceptance increases every day, we still have made only a start. We've come through the cold winter, as it were, and reached the spring; the long summer of growth toward total acceptance is still ahead."*

In the Mainstream to Stay

Today's disabled are finding their way into the major currents of life in a manner no less spectacular than the famous disabled who went before them. Like Helen Keller and Franklin Delano Roosevelt, who are remembered for their remarkable success in overcoming tremendous odds, our present-day achievers are proving to be unstoppable.

Choosing not to remain in the background any longer, they are busy getting laws changed, climbing city hall steps, earning degrees, teaching karate, being senators, administering large federal agencies, composing songs, painting pictures, writing books, patenting inventions, running their own businesses.

Roy Campanella has been a quadriplegic since 1958, when an auto accident ended his colorful

* *A World To Care For* (New York, Random House, 1972), p. 281.

baseball career with the then Brooklyn Dodgers. Mr. Campanella is now an active businessman who goes to his office every day, keeps tabs on the sports world, and travels extensively. Soon after his accident, the Campanellas purchased an existing suburban New York home and planned its access modifications. A small interior elevator, which Mr. Campanella says is one of his best investments, permits him to reach, unaided, the basement, garage, and patio as well as main-floor level. Here, there is a large, fully accessible kitchen of Mrs. Campanella's design, and a master suite containing bedroom, bath, and private study. Roy and Roxie Campanella go out to restaurants and theaters and take frequent ocean cruises and flights to the West Coast. Whenever they make reservations, they also ask about accessibility: number of steps, presence of ramps, steepness of aisles. Their advice to the disabled who like to visit places far and near: plan ahead. "Restaurants and theater managers, ship lines, and especially the airlines are nice to us," he says, "but we always check with them in advance."

Max Cleland, triple amputee, former Georgia state senator, and present administrator of the Veterans Administration, identifies with the disabled and is in a position to bring their needs into legislative perspective. He authored the first bill in Georgia to make public places accessible to the disabled; it was signed into law by then Governor Carter in 1972. Mr. Cleland believes that freeing buildings for the disabled makes them more accessible to the population in general. Ramps, for instance, are not exclusive, they are inclusive; they benefit not only one group of people but all of them. He says he'd like to see more forethought used during the planning stages to determine how accessible a building or public complex is likely to be to all who may wish to use it; it would save a lot of time later. Mr. Cleland lives in a Washington, D.C., apartment that he says is roomy enough not to need special access modifications. For those who fear releasing a child or adult into the mainstream, his message is "Let go and let God."

With representatives such as these, the disabled will not only make an important place for themselves in the mainstream but will enrich it considerably.

Where in the World

Last year the United Nations estimated that 10 percent of the world's population is sufficiently disabled to require special services. That amounts to 400 million people who need access to public buildings and thoroughfares, functional housing, and transportation, as well as to such aspects of mainstream living as education, communications, nutrition, clothing, health care, jobs, and recreation.

Programs and services set up for the disabled throughout the world are as different in size, scope, and method of delivery as there are differences in governments and national attitudes.

European systems, for example, tend to be comprehensive, highly standardized, and widely distributed. Although methods of funding and administering these services vary from country to country, there are three concepts at the heart of Europe's programs that are fundamentally the same. First, services are designed to keep the disabled and family together and functioning as a viable unit within the community. Second, home-help services are considered essential for implementing this philosophy. Third, home-help services, financed or subsidized by the government, are a respected profession that men and women are willing to enter and be identified with.

Home-help services are not geared strictly to patient health-care needs but include maintaining and improving the family's capability to stay together and continue its regular routine and daily pursuits; homemaking, shopping, and time for recreation are all considered essential if the alternative—institutional care—is to be avoided.

Asia, on the other hand, has no compre-

hensive network of services, and very few programs have been devised to train or mainstream the disabled. The few that have gotten under way were initiated by concerned individuals or small coalitions of the disabled who sustain the programs on their own without government subsidy.

Being largely rural and having enormous populations, Asia's nations are faced with solving a staggering number of daily living problems before they can even begin to address the question of the disabled. Among them, only Japan seems to be on its way toward recognizing and meeting their needs.

The Tokyo metropolitan government last spring began to urge banks, department stores, and transportation systems to modify their facilities for access by the disabled. At the same time, the city itself began to renovate a number of hospitals and public buildings according to a new group of standards devised for all future structures funded by the Tokyo government.

Once In, Then What?

Whether the programs and services devised by the nations of the world for their disabled citizens are comprehensive, haphazard, or almost nonexistent, one common goal appears to dominate them all: keep the disabled in the mainstream, not separated from family and community behind institutional walls.

As this attitude continues to gain momentum, there will be an increasing need to bring the disabled consumer into closer touch with the goods and services he or she needs to make independent living possible. In this respect, disabled Americans are at a disadvantage, for despite our incredible productivity, there's a decided lack of information about where to find products. The first effort ever made in this country to remedy that situation occurred in the summer of 1977. An International Disabled

Exposition was organized by the Paralyzed Veterans of America and supported by other groups of disabled persons. Most of the exhibitors in the first exposition, held in Chicago, were manufacturers of medical aids, but the PVA is aiming to make future shows more inclusive and representative of the full range of goods the disabled include in their lives: home furnishings, housewares, clothing, personal-care items, cars, vans, recreational vehicles, mobile homes, airplanes, electronically activated devices for home and office.

In contrast, Europe's disabled have two advantages over those in this country: prices are kept within reasonable limits (because, in many instances, aids and equipment for the disabled are furnished free or at subsidized prices by the government); and various information services send lists of available products to the disabled and maintain product displays in several areas throughout the country.

One, sponsored by the Disabled Living Foundation in London, managed by its Information Service division and called the Aids Centre, is located at 346 Kensington High Street, London W14 8NS, London, England. The Centre contains a permanent display of a comprehensive range of aids for disabled people of all ages living in their own homes or other domestic settings.

The disabled and their relatives are welcome to visit the Centre, and while the items on display are not for sale, complete information on sources of supply, cost, and the like is available.

The Centre shows a wide range of products and useful information, such as:

Photographic display of suitable architectural features; portable ramps, handrails, signs

Washing aids including toothbrushes, towels, soap holders, bathmats, and razors; taps, various types of bath seats; specially designed bathtubs; shower seats; toilet aids and raised toilet seats

Commodes and bed pans; protective clothing and appliances for the control of incontinence

Beds—adjustable in height, sit-you-up, and stand-you-up; bedclothing and anti-pressure-sore material and equipment

Clothing, both ready-made and adapted; dressing aids

Tables and chairs; reading and writing aids; communication aids; telephone aids and adaptations; indicators and alarm systems; indoor recreation; music

Eating and drinking aids; aids for the preparation, cooking, and serving of food; laundry aids such as washing machines, tumbler dryers, irons, and drying racks

Cleaning aids, dustpans, brushes, mops, and vacuum cleaners; sink units and working surfaces, cookers of various types; trolleys, trays, and mats; refrigerators and storage shelving; small electric appliances

Wheelchairs—self-propelling, push, and electric; sticks, crutches, and walking frames; wheelchair accessories, such as covers, trays, and cushions; hoists, freestanding and overhead; car conversions; aids for the disabled driver and passenger

According to Susan Grant, administrative assistant of the Disabled Living Foundation Information Service, the Aids Centre, to get started, wrote to manufacturers to ask if they would lend their products for display. (The foundation's files contained a good cross section of equipment available in Britain.) The Centre always reserves the right to send back equipment when it wishes to change displays. Also, staff members keep their eyes open for information about new products.

Now that the Centre is well known, Miss Grant says, "Many manufacturers will send us details of new products, either before they are on the market or as soon as they become available. Manufacturers are usually keen that we have information about their products in our main files and on our information lists. They are also always keen that, if possible, their products are on display in the Aids Centre."

Chapter 13

Getting Around

One fine day in the spring of 1976, the citizens of a West Coast city were startled to see a number of their disabled neighbors leaving their wheelchairs and crawling up the city hall steps. The group was slowly making its way to a city council meeting being held in a room several flights up to protest the building's and thereby the council's, inaccessibility.

For years, the disabled have been unable to exercise their right to participate in public affairs because of limited access to the community's thoroughfares and meeting places. Little by little the scene is begining to change. Civic leaders in cities and towns are being prodded, mostly by the disabled themselves, into reshaping their attitudes about the disabled in general, and city planning in particular.

Sensitivity to their needs is growing, as the disabled will find as they encounter pockets of progress here and there. By no means is the atmosphere of change, or the activity toward it, cohesive or widespread. But since a drive toward accomplishment has begun, you should be aware of what and where some of the advances are if for no other reason than to let you know

you are not totally alone in efforts to make independent living a reality.

In Cincinnati's downtown shopping district, the sidewalks have curb-cut ramps (with handrails) situated, not at the corners, but adjacent to the regular flow of pedestrian traffic.

The city of San Francisco is building ramps at crosswalks in every neighborhood shopping area, in the downtown shopping district, and in the civic center. Begun three years ago, the project will continue for four more years until it is complete. It was initiated, incidentally, by a group of disabled persons who banded together and called themselves the Coalition for the Removal of Architectural Barriers (CRAB).*

Getting around in one's own car is, for the physically disabled, a major necessity. Many cities and towns have reserved-parking spaces, marked with the international symbol of access for handicapped motorists. But all too often other drivers don't notice, or disregard, the special parking rule, and use the spaces for themselves. In Alabama, the Governor's Com-

* *Report,* May/June 1976, newsletter published by the National Center for a Barrier-Free Environment.

mittee on Employment of the Handicapped has produced books of tickets to issue to such thoughtless drivers, admonishing them for blocking spaces reserved for the disabled and asking for their future consideration.*

All Southern New England Telephone Company public coin-phone installations now are being installed 54 in./1,372 mm above ground level, a more convenient height for wheelchair users. This break from tradition was announced last year to a volunteer task-force group concerned with architectural barriers known as EACH (Equal Access Concerns for the Handicapped) in the greater Bridgeport, Connecticut, area.†

From sidewalks to college classrooms, from public telephones to airports, the slow process of reshaping begins. City, state, and federal officials cite lax enforcement of antidiscrimination and access laws, funding, and inflexible attitudes about the disabled on the part of many nondisabled as the major barriers they have to surmount. They are predicting no timetable for full accomplishment, though they do agree that until the disabled, their families, and friends went on the move, very little was done. Now decisions are being made and implemented at a rate that surprises them.

Public transportation systems, on the other hand, can't report much in the way of progress toward the solution to a very knotty problem: the disabled have the fare but they can't get on the bus, or train, or subway.

The disabled and elderly view this failure to provide them with accessible public transportation as a form of discrimination, since their only alternative is to use segregated transportation or private means which are expensive yet limited in range and scheduling.

A great controversy is brewing over how best to redesign public-transit vehicles and who will make the new carriers once the dimensions are settled. Those who manufacture vehicles say a

new design would mean they'd have to retool and pass on the extra costs and that nobody wants that. Somebody else figured out that making new vehicles would not cost as much as it now does in disability and welfare benefits to subsidize people who cannot support themselves because they can't get on the bus and go to work every day.

Again this is an oversimplified appraisal of a complex issue, but since no solutions seem about to occur very soon, you'd do well to look around for your own way out. Only in this case, keep a close eye on what's going on and join the disabled in their efforts to have the issue properly resolved; a poorly conceived course of action on the part of the decision makers could affect all of us, financially or otherwise.

Personal Transportation

The family car can be outfitted with special drive controls so that the person with limited mobility can drive himself, or you and the disabled could consider a wheelchair van equipped with suitable lift and control devices. Check the Yellow Pages for firms that handle van sales and conversions. If there is no such listing for your area, ask your favorite auto dealer. He should be able to tell you or find out for you from the manufacturer that makes the cars he sells. Prices can be high, up to ten thousand dollars or more, depending upon the kind and sophistication of equipment and options chosen.

Outfitting the family car with special drive controls is far less costly. One group of controls you could consider are those designed and sold by a disabled driver and available from Nelson Medical Products, 5690 Sarah Avenue, Sarasota, Florida 33581 (see Figure 13-1).

Auto-mate (A), for one-hand driving and finger-tip control, fits all American cars and most foreign makes. It comes with instructions and diagrams so that you can install it yourself. Complete with dimmer switch, it costs $125.

* Ibid.
† Ibid.

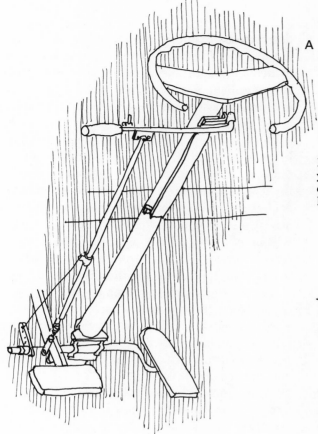

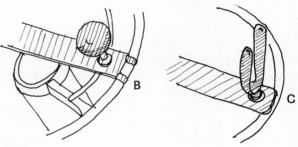

13–1 Drive controls and attachments you can install yourself, all by Nelson Medical: (A) Auto-mate, for one-hand driving; (B) quadriplegic spinner bar; (C) hand fits into open-top loop.

The quadriplegic spinner bar (B) is engineered for those who have difficulty grasping a steering wheel. It clamps securely inside the wheel and is designed to hold one of the many knobs, rings, or cuffs Mr. Nelson makes for varied disabilities. The bar shown is $18; the knob attachment is $12.

The open-top loop attachment (C) fits the spinner bar, and permits the hand to slip in with little effort. The price is $12.

Travel: Near Places

As towns and cities begin to open up for easier access, so too does the world, in a sense. Greater opportunities exist now for travel than have previously been available to those with limited mobility.

Overseas travel by air and sea is giving their lives a new rich dimension as the world's most fascinating countries are making their hotels, restaurants, and scenic wonders more and more accessible each year.

Here at home, the disabled will find a rich and growing assortment of places to see and visit, such as:

Wheelchair Vacationing in the Black Hills and Badlands of South Dakota: Guide Booklet for the Handicapped. Available from the Black Hills, Badlands, and Lakes Association, P.O. Box 539, Sturgis, South Dakota 57785.

Wheeling Through Wheeling. Available from the Wheeling–Ohio County Planning Commission, Room 305, City-County Building, 1600 Chapline Street, Wheeling, West Virginia 26003.

Both of these plus many more American and European listings are in a guidebook available to you for the asking. Write for *A list of Guide-books for Handicapped Travelers*, The Women's Committee, The President's Committee on Employment of the Handicapped, Washington, D.C. 20210.

For information on the accessibility of our parks and recreational areas write the Committee on Recreation and Leisure, the President's Committee on Employment of the Handicapped, Washington, D.C. 20210.

For a more personal touch, investigate membership in a nonprofit travel club designed especially for the disabled and managed by the founder of Handy-Cap Horizons, Inc., Dorothy S. Axsom. Mrs. Axsom arranges group tours for the members, who number about three thousand and pay dues of $6 to $25 per year. For details about membership and how the groups are organized, send a stamped, self-addressed envelope to Mrs. Dorothy S. Axsom, 3250 East Loretta Drive, Indianapolis, Indiana 46227.

Airlines are showing increasing concern for and understanding of disabled passengers, although there is still some controversy over a recent FAA ruling that permits individual airlines to set their own procedures for accepting passengers who may require help during evacuation in an emergency. To some, this permits arbitrary decision making on the part of an airline bordering on infringement of one's right to make his own choice in the matter of travel. The new ruling does make other areas of service and responsibility more clear. They are: flight attendants must individually brief the disabled passenger and any accompanying attendant on safety and evacuation procedures, and must ask the appropriate way to assist the passenger in order to avoid causing him pain or injury. Canes and crutches still cannot be kept at the individual's seat (the reason is possible damage to evacuation chutes and the like), and disabled travelers still can be refused passage if they fail to give the airline proper advance notice of their intention to travel with the airline.

All major airlines consulted showed, by their description of procedures and services, that they are making substantial and conscientious efforts to accommodate the disabled in a responsible and dignified way. Isolated problems do crop up from time to time, but no more for the disabled than the nondisabled.

One tip from a long-time traveler is worth keeping in mind. If your trip will involve use of more than one airline, check out the arrangements each requires and the accommodations each can provide. This helps assure you that the arrangements you made at the start of the flight will be effective all along the route. A seasoned traveler checks flights through to the end; it is even more imperative for the disabled to do so.

TWA has just developed an enclosed elevator-type lift for transporting wheelchair users traveling on narrow-body aircraft through airports that do not have jetways. Passengers board the lift at the terminal door, are driven to planeside, and are elevated to proper height for boarding in their own wheelchairs. Specially designed narrow wheelchairs are used on board the aircraft when necessary.

Travel: Far Places

Guidebooks for disabled visitors to other lands are appearing at a rapid rate. Some of the latest are of interest, though it must be mentioned that they are not all free.

Belgium   *A National Guide to Public Buildings Accessible to the Disabled.* Available from Croix-Rouge de Belgique, Chaussé de Vieguat, 98, 1050 Bruxelles, Belgium. Price: 50 BF.

Denmark   *A Hotel Guide for the Handicapped.* Available from The Society and Home for the Disabled, 34 Esplanaden, DK-1263, Copenhagen, K, Denmark. Price: $4.00 (includes airmail postage).

France   A guide for disabled travelers is available from publisher Imprimerie du Midi, 18 Bd. Felix Mercader, 66004 Perpignan, France. Price: 32 francs plus postage.

Switzerland *Hotel Guide for the Disabled,* Swiss Invalid Association, Froburgstrasse 4, 4000 Olten, Switzerland. No price listed.

United   (England, Northern Ireland, Scotland, Wales) *Holidays for the Physically Handicapped,* The Central Council for the Disabled, 34 Eccleston Square, London SW1V1 1PE, England. Price: $1.00.
Kingdom

West   A 1977 vacation guide, *Hilfe für Behinderte,* is available from the publisher, Bundesarbeitsgemeinschaft, e.V., Kirchfeldstr. 149, 4000, Dusseldorf, Germany. No price listed.
Germany

CHAPTER 14

Designs for Living

Able-bodied family members have needs, too. It's natural that many of them drop everything to rush to the injured person's side during the early days and weeks of the emergency. Later on, as the months pass, attitudes begin to shift as lines to the outer world—jobs, school, friends, the community—are reconnected.

Knowing the pattern of their lives will be changed in some way by the disability that has befallen one of them, each family member eventually begins to establish his or her own mode of life. Some make their adjustments more comfortably than others.

In interviews with families about how they found release from pressure both for themselves and a disabled child or adult, it was apparent that those who encourage the drive toward self-sufficiency in the disabled won an extra measure of freedom for themselves as well. Also, they joined in helping the disabled set up an independent life-style, whether it happened to be at home, in an apartment across town, or in a distant city.

Letting Go

Susan L.: "I know our friends thought we'd lost our minds when they realized my husband and I were serious about letting our son, Jim, get an apartment of his own. Jim was twenty-two at the time and a paraplegic. He'd been hurt in a diving accident two years before.

"That first year after the accident was a nightmare for all of us: Jim, his two older sisters, his father, and me. But somewhere along the way Jim got so wrapped up in his therapy at the treatment center that he began to seem like his old outgoing, friendly self. He'd always been athletic, so his exercises and training meant something special to him.

"His father and I, though, were a mess. We knocked ourselves out trying to keep so busy and not worry that we worried ourselves sick. Really sick. By the time Jim was home to stay, his father and I were so supercharged with concern over Jim's future and our roles in it, we became overprotective.

114

"Jim could hardly stand it, although none of us realized what we were doing at the time. I just know that at first Jim was glad to be home and show us all the things he could do. There were a couple of setbacks that winter and he had to go in for more treatment. Each time he came back home we were more uptight, we wouldn't leave him for a minute. We didn't go anywhere or see anybody for nearly a year. Jim got sullen, then very, very quiet.

"All of a sudden, it was around Christmas, he started losing his temper over the smallest things. When his sisters and their families came in from out of state, just for one day, he was impossible. Finally Janet, my oldest daughter, shouted back at Jim, something like 'Maybe you'd like to go live somewhere else' and Jim said, 'Yeah, I'd like that, I'd really like that.' Well, I was stunned. I didn't think he meant it. What would he do? How would he do?

"It took a while to sink in, but my husband and I finally got around to asking Jim about it. We also discussed it with his doctor. Then we talked about it with anyone who'd listen. Finally we said we'd give it a try. As soon as we convinced ourselves and Jim that we were serious, he changed completely. He began to look better and feel better. It took a while to find a place, but while Jim was at the treatment center, he met people with places of their own, so they gave him leads.

"Jim's in college now, catching up on his education. He lives near the campus, almost ninety miles from here. We don't see him often, and I still wake up in the middle of the night worrying about him. I guess that's natural. Letting go isn't ever easy. But I would tell any parent who asked: Do it, and the sooner you can let them try it on their own, the better."

Take Time for Rest and Recreation

If your own or the disabled person's doctor or therapist tells you to get more rest, or suggests you get out more, take the advice. Your first impulse might be to get angry since they don't tell you how to accomplish it. With all you have to do, how can they expect you to drop everything to relax and play? You might well ask, but sooner or later, as you are about to reach the breaking point, you will find a way.

Many a good book, later made into a movie, began as a therapeutic way out of just this kind of dilemma. Other books, poems, short stories, and songs, which will never rest on a publisher's desk, have been written for the same reason. And in the doing, new perspectives were formed, unexpressed tensions dissolved.

Creative arts aren't the only outlet. Many parents who have a disabled child or aged relative living at home have a standing arrangement with a friend or neighbor to sit in for them at regular times each week or month. The regularity of these free times is important, for it gives the adults something specific to look forward to, and it lets the child or elderly person know that while his family will not always be around, they nevertheless aren't pulling away from him or her unexpectedly.

Often, family members who do not have a job are encouraged to find part-time work or volunteer for some community effort. One mother of a disabled youngster works as a cub reporter for a local newspaper. Another gives piano lessons in her students' homes. Another serves as a teacher's aide in the nearby grade school. All of them establish a regular working schedule and stick to it, barring emergencies, so that the double-edged sword of dependency doesn't become too firmly embedded in their daily lives.

Travel is another way to break through the restrictions imposed on daily living when one member is limited by physical impairment. Adults, especially, find it a refreshing outlet. Thanks to new attitudes about travel for the disabled, and the vehicles and services that now help make it possible, more couples, and whole families, are adding a new dimension to their lives by leaving home whenever they can.

•

It Has to Be Told

Independent living is a two-way street. Yet when society says, You have no right to abandon this disabled child or adult, or, You must see to his every need, the nondisabled suddenly find their psyches falling apart. Some turn their lives around so completely they cease to exist for anything except the disabled individual. Husbands and wives forget the life they once had; children drift about on the periphery. Or the opposite may happen. The urge to turn and run the other way is overpowering. Few will, or can, react in a way that allows objective focus upon the changes in life-style that the accident or illness has brought about.

At the same time, the disabled individual, unless very young, is in despair about his now and future life and is looking for answers from anyone who might be able to give them. Once the shock waves pass, everyone involved is in some form of active or passive chaos.

Then begins, within the nondisabled, a bub-

bling up of feelings that will be difficult to cope with: fear, resentment, bitterness, disappointment, frustration, anger, exhaustion. Confusion takes hold in a way that seems to block true expression of anguish. Furthermore, there's an unconscious attempt to smother such feelings on the grounds that they are unacceptable and unforgivable.

Everyone who's gone through what you are now facing has felt the same way, in different degrees of intensity, for different lengths of time. No one, doctors and psychiatrists believe, ever escapes such reactions.

How you deal with them has to be up to you, but those who are close to people in these situations advise that you talk it out with some person or group with whom you feel comfortable. Since you have a right, as it were, to feel afraid or angry or overburdened, you have a right to express it. The sooner you can do this, say the professionals in the field of rehabilitation medicine, the sooner you and the disabled will begin to design your lives on a foundation of personal freedom and independence.

Chapter **15**

Getting Help

Buy a small notebook, a pen, some plain stationery with envelopes, and a book of stamps. Carry the notebook with you wherever you go. Jot down the names, addresses and telephone numbers (zip and area codes, too) of the people you encounter at the treatment center who are visiting a child or adult with a disability similar to the one affecting your friend or relative.

These men and women can become the nucleus of a personal share-your-problem group. Because of privacy laws, you cannot obtain lists of disabled persons with whom to exchange ideas and talk out experiences. Other than stopping someone on the street, the best way to meet those in a situation like your own is right there in the hospital.

At the large treatment centers, you'll find people from all parts of the country, even the world. In due time they return to their homes, and you may never see them again unless you establish contact as soon as possible. Having someone to talk to and correspond with is a way of getting a kind of help that no special service agency can provide.

Also, keep a separate list of the official organizations—federal, state, and local—designed to serve the disabled to which you have been referred by doctors or that you hear about. Get names and complete addresses. Don't be satisfied by such vague directions as "Go to that big building down the street" or "Drop by the mayor's office. Someone there can probably help you."

Wherever possible, get the telephone number of the agency or organization and the name of a person to whom you can speak. When you call to arrange an appointment, or get information, tell the person who answers exactly what it is you want: you're trying to find a school for a disabled child; or you want to know what financial aid is available to one in your situation; or you want to apply for special benefits.

If you're required to go to the agency in person, find out what cards, forms, numbers, or papers you should bring with you in order to discuss the situation. You'll save your own precious time and energy if you have all the necessary documents on the first visit. Otherwise, you'll have to make another trip.

Even then, getting help from public and private agencies will be a trying experience. Being prepared with the proper documents will smooth your way somewhat. Courteous persistence will do a great deal, too, for there's much confusion out there.

If all the organizations interested in, dedicated to, created for, and concerned with the disabled could be counted, the number would be staggering. Get that: *if* the number could be counted. At this writing, no one person, publication, or group knows how many such organizations exist in the country at the moment.

You might well say, "Great, with so much activity and solicitude there must be a lot of help around!" In total, there is. But, as with getting oil out of an underground deposit and into the home furnace, there's many a slippery plank along the way. Anyone in the business has a proprietary interest in his or her part of the process—from the smallest valve to the largest supertanker.

Out of the gigantic effort to ease the burdens that physical impairment places upon individual and community has grown a tangled, duplicated, triplicated skein of red tape so vast it imposes new problems on top of the ones it's designed to solve.

Perhaps something is happening now that eventually will make a viable network of aid for the disabled out of the mammoth snarl that presently looms before us.

President Carter, in an address to the disabled attending the White House Conference on Handicapped Individuals in Washington, D.C., on May 24, 1977, said his administration would reorganize programs for the disabled into one agency.

At that conference, also, parents of the disabled made it known that they wanted a more active part in the formulation of legislation and policies that affect their and their children's lives.

For the first time in our history the disabled, their families, and the administration are vocal and on the move to face and seek solutions to problems that have hidden and grown in the dark for too long.

Such a massive readjustment of ongoing attitudes and practices will require tremendous amounts of effort, patience, understanding—and time.

Right now, only disabled veterans and their families have access to comprehensive services from one organization, the Veterans Administration. Since 1930 it has been set up to provide health care, housing, educational, and vocational assistance to veterans and their dependents.

"At present," says Administrator Max Cleland, "the VA serves over two million veterans with service-connected disabilities plus nearly three million more men, women, and children who are eligible for the help we can give them."

Without a link to the Veterans Administration, other disabled and concerned families and friends have to rely on one highly overused resource—themselves. But what a free and unrestricted source of power it is. If used in a positive rather than negative way, your self-reliance can help and comfort you.

In addition to forming a mutual sharing system with people who've been where you are now, read the tips and experiences that others have to offer. Subscribe to such publications as:

Accent on Living
P.O. Box 700
Gillum Road & High Drive
Bloomington, Illinois 61701

Rehabilitation Gazette
4502 Maryland Avenue
St. Louis, Missouri 63108

From each of these you will get tips on coping, personal experiences, leads to products, ideas you can adapt, as well as information about legislation and services. Written for and by the disabled, they will afford you valuable insight into the ways and means of independent living.

Become a catalogue collector. Save yourself from running around in frustrating searches for things that you need, or might need. Have catalogues from medical supply firms, department stores, mass merchandisers such as Sears, JC Penney, Wards, Spiegel. Gather housewares, hardware, and furniture catalogues; boat supply catalogues (many a good compact kitchen there); electrical- and electronic-supply catalogues.

Occasionally pick up copies of special-interest magazines sold at newsstands on such subjects as boating, recreational vehicles, mobile homes, cars and motorcycles (for ramps that may be advertised), camping (for safety, lighting, cooking ideas). How-to magazines will give helpful tips on home repair, remodeling, and sources of new products.

One publication you should have is entitled *A Handbook on the Legal Rights of Handicapped People.* Write the Superintendent of Documents, U.S. Government Printing Office, Washington, D.C. 20402. The price is $1.80 per copy.

Comprehensive information on how the disabled can obtain their legal rights as citizens as well as consumers is clearly explained in a book by Lilly Bruck, *Access: A Guide to a Better Life for Disabled Americans* (New York: Random House, 1978), currently in bookstores.

Another is *Social Services '75. A Citizen's Handbook.* Write to the Rehabilitation Services Administration, U.S. Department of Health, Education, and Welfare, Washington, D.C. 20201. In addition to outlining the various services you or the disabled may be eligible for, the booklet contains information on the Social Security Administration's Supplemental Income program for providing cash assistance to needy aged, blind, and disabled people.

An Extra Pair of Hands

One of the most important additions to any household, whether the disabled lives alone or with his or her family, is a full-time or part-time attendant. Such men and women can mean the difference between freedom and total dependency upon state, community, or relatives; without them the possibility looms of an institutional life that can do little more than provide a corner from which the disabled watches one day pass into the next.

Finding an attendant may well seem an exercise in futility, for in this country there exists a strange paradox: we're an altruistic breed claiming great compassion for the welfare of others, but when it comes to the daily nitty-gritty of doing for others, nobody's there. Unfortunately, the distance between our professions of concern and our acts is ample and empty. As a result, caring becomes a legal responsibility which falls upon one or two individuals without letup until each reaches a breaking point; then the public must take over.

Yet the public is straining on the one hand to support an increasing number of people who have no work to do, while on the other it strives to support those who can't find someone to work for them. This is a crudely oversimplified view of a complex situation, but it illustrates, nonetheless, the odd gap between our problems and our solutions.

No one denies that helping another in the day-after-day routine of personal care is a task that must be shared, for otherwise the emotional and physical reservoir of the giver quickly runs dry.

Nor should it be supposed any longer that this task is a moral obligation that must be fulfilled without respite or remuneration. Too many families have been torn apart, too many disabled children and adults abandoned to public care, simply because a relative or friend knew, or feared, that he or she couldn't carry the burden alone and without rest or access to a personal life.

Bringing those who need something to do into contact with those who want to hire them is difficult because each group seems to be unaware of the other's existence. But finding someone to be a part-time or live-in attendant is not impossible, though it does take persistence and ingenuity. The line in this instance is more important than the bait. Given the very real possibility that there is both need and want, the object is to bring the two groups together. Active communication is the quickest route. You know what you want, so ask around. Explore private sources before you attempt public ones, simply because of the time and frustration that will be involved in the latter.

Newspaper advertisements are one of the most direct methods. Another is to write or call local church groups and leaders. Fraternal and civic organizations such as Rotary and Kiwanis clubs or YM and YWCAs may know of someone who could help out. Get in touch with high school and college counselors for leads to students who are looking for part-time work.

There's nothing wrong with stopping a perfect stranger and asking if he or she knows of someone, provided your approach is dignified rather than pleading.

Fire and police departments in small cities and towns may have helpful suggestions (metropolitan police and fire departments are too busy to cope with anything but emergencies).

Home-extension-service representatives, members of the local Salvation Army, and the local librarian may all be able to make suggestions. County social workers and the unemployment office are frequently sources of help. The Visiting Nurses' Service is another.

Select Carefully

An attendant must be chosen with great care, for you are asking two human beings, the disabled individual and the aide, to share very personal aspects of life and home.

Above all, the interview and selection of an attendant must be done by the disabled individual (unless that person is too young or unable for some reason to make such decisions). Their personalities must complement rather than oppose each other; some trial and error may be experienced before settling in takes place. Compensation and time off must be agreeably worked out and adhered to. Anyone hired solely for the care of a disabled person should not be expected or asked to perform special duties for other members of the household unless this has been clearly established as part of the paid working relationship.

Given time, patience, and proper matching of people, the bond between attendant and disabled can form a chain of miracles for family and community.

Chapter 16

An Unfinished Script

Huge, firmly established businesses, private agencies, and publicly funded social institutions exist to supply goods and services to the disabled through channels that differ from those serving nondisabled mass-market consumers. Automatic doors, for instance, are made for big-budget institutions and municipal projects but not for private residences. A bicycle tire that also fits certain wheelchairs was once sold in local bicycle shops. Now all such tires are available only through medical supply firms, which obtain them from one source that controls distribution of this particular tire. Thick, easy-to-grasp, attractively styled door handles can be bought through architects and contractors but not in the hardware store down the street.

There are two supply lines: one for the commercial or contract market—which still identifies the disabled as its customers, however indirect—and one for the everyday shopping-center patron. Both systems are working smoothly and contributing to the gross national product in an orderly way. Neither is capable of shifting to a new system quickly; to do so would seriously threaten the balance of our economic framework. Many sound, thriving businesses employing hundreds of thousands of people are geared for this two-market approach. Traditions as firmly rooted as these will be difficult to change.

But change they must, because the disabled are not in institutions where they once were; they are outside in the mainstream, living, working, and striving like everyone else.

Medical science, rehabilitation techniques, and a revolutionary fervor on the part of the disabled to break through old attitudinal barriers have all combined to produce a new group of consumer-citizens who have separated from and outdistanced their usual lines of supply.

There's much catching up to do. But manufacturers don't know where the disabled are or what they need; the disabled and you, their concerned supporters, don't know how to reach the producers of products. What's more, even public agencies designed to serve the needs of the disabled admit that many are not aware of the services that are available to them. Communications seem to have broken down between the disabled and the government; between the disabled and industry.

Perhaps an overhaul of the massive federal complex will help mend the break. With President Carter's pledge to reorganize services for the disabled into one system, combined with pressures from the disabled for a direct voice in the legislative process, the move toward a more positive link between supply and demand could begin.

Then, if bridges between the disabled consumer and manufacturers of products could be built, another needless communications gap would be closed.

What Industry Could Do

To reach the disabled, industries can use the communications networks they've been using for decades: their advertising, sales promotion, and public relations operations.

Even more communications power can be harnessed by using the many trade associations that are affiliated with each industry: home building, home remodeling, home furnishings, appliances, equipment and fixtures; passenger and recreation vehicles; mobile homes; electronic equipment—to name a few.

Some of these associations are influential both nationally and locally. They are well-staffed and have healthy budgets. They publish magazines and newsletters for their membership; conduct demographic and marketing surveys; have sophisticated electronic information storage and retrieval systems.

Even smaller trade associations that are primarily one- and two-person operations never-

theless have access to a cohesive network of members who are makers and distributors of enormous quantities of goods and services that the public needs and wants.

The high-impact industry trade shows which link manufacturers with the vendors of their products, who in turn present these goods to the public, offer tremendous communications potential. These shows draw together as many as 500 to 60,000 members at a clip. They meet in workshops and seminars to learn about and discuss all phases of their industry. Their interests range from the knottiest legislative problem to the best-selling ball bearing. What better time and place (with little or no increase in association budget) is there for manufacturers, distributors, and retailers to meet with the disabled and discuss mutual problems face to face? What better opportunity for the disabled to reach hundreds, even thousands, of industry representatives than through a few articulate disabled spokespersons at these industry gatherings?

Industry can do even more, still at no increase in budget. Consumer test panels, for instance, used by some large companies to determine customer response to particular products, could and should include the disabled—not as a separate group but as part of the total representative assembly. The role of the disabled in such a test panel should be one of understanding and assistance: to suggest, along with the nondisabled, how a product will benefit the largest number of people, nondisabled and disabled alike.

What the Disabled Can Do

The disabled are taking charge of their affairs in ways that will undoubtedly make them easier to see and target for marketing attention. Simply by appearing in protest lines and demonstration marches, they've made their presence known. But they will also need to communicate with producers of goods and providers of services in a direct and positive way. This means, however, that disabled men and women should do the talking; it should not be done for them by able-bodied representatives of agencies or institutions. The disabled are quite capable of speaking for themselves and should do so.

Industry may not yet have found a way to reach the disabled, but the disabled can certainly reach industry. You and the disabled can write to company presidents to make your wants and needs known. You don't even have to know his name. Just write President, Such and Such Company, and the address.

If you want to reach an entire group of manufacturers, write the director of the trade association it is likely to be affiliated with. Call or walk into any established store or business and ask for the name and address of the association, be it one involved with furniture, kitchen appliances, or cars. Let the association know, by letter, that the disabled are customers, too; that you and they have certain needs that are not being attended to, and that you are herewith making those needs known.

If enough of you make yourselves heard, action can begin. But nothing will happen if you don't speak up.

The disabled are not asking for specially designed products per se. They are asking what products are available and where, in the mainstream, they can be obtained—at competitive prices.

Here, the disabled will need the support of the nondisabled in their efforts to dislodge some important products and services from supply lines too carefully hidden from the influences of competitive pricing. Practices involved in the sale and repair of wheelchairs, mechanical lifts, and automatic devices for private homes and passenger vehicles need a thorough airing.

Your line of action in this skirmish will be toward the legislative, for until the pressure you bring upon your own elected officials is heavy enough to offset that being used by those interested in preserving the closeted sources of supply, little will be done to let the force of competitive pricing do its work.

Breaking Other Barriers

Consumer publishing has managed to ignore the entire issue of disability for decades, yet this country's magazines and newspapers could do more than any other segment of mass communication to bring the needs and accomplishments of the disabled into national focus. Letters to the editor are one way to press for recognition, but it is wise to be aware that altruism dictates few editorial policies; advertising money does more. Rather than rail against this philosophy, you will do better to use it as leverage: pressure upon industry to respond to the disabled as valuable customers can result in an approach to consumer advertising and sales promotion which can't help but trigger responsiveness from publishers.

Other legislative reforms that need to be addressed are those dealing with hiring the disabled, home-care and attendant services, and taxation.

The disabled need jobs, and the law says they must be considered for employment. Be aware, then, of the laws that prohibit discrimination. If your friend or relative is job-hunting, make it your business to see them through this tiring ritual; lend your own outrage if things don't seem to be on the up and up.

By all means, have a copy of *A Handbook on the Legal Rights of Handicapped People*, mentioned in the preceding chapter. Also, The President's Committee on Employment of the Handicapped, Washington, D.C., 20210, will send you additional information if you request it in writing.

The practices and attitudes surrounding home-care services need a complete overhaul and fresh approach. Perhaps certain aspects of the European method could be adopted. However, care will have to be taken in this country to keep such a system, admittedly utopian, as free of bureaucratic interference as possible. Not an easy task, for in two hundred years we have edged away from our early spirit of independence and developed in its place a take-care-of-me attitude. This has made us all too willing to give our problems over to someone else to handle—in this case, the government. As a result, taxes have risen to the point where even those who shun being dependent can't afford not to be. Tax incentives, therefore, need to be designed that will encourage private-family-home and mainstream living, easing the enormous drain on public funds now used to sustain institutional life.

Nobody's Perfect

If numbers tell a company president, state governor, or village mayor anything, they reveal the profile of a nation that is hardly flawless.

Of the 210 million of us—and at the present rate of birth, death, calamity, and luck—20 million are elderly, 17 million are under the age of five, 19 million are between the ages of six

and thirteen, and 2 million are pregnant. That's 58 million citizens who are up and walking around with varying degrees of speed and accuracy.

There are 11.7 million physically disabled, 12 million laid up temporarily by injury, 2.4 million deaf, 11 million with impaired hearing. 1.3 million blind, 8.2 million with visual impairment, 6.8 million mentally retarded, 1.7 million homebound, and 2.1 million in assorted institutions, or a total of 57.2 million who don't catch the news or go shopping every day; leaving 95 million out of 210 million who function in what is regarded as a normal manner.

Perhaps such statistics, compiled by the National Endowment for the Arts in 1976, will put into perspective the size of the disabled population in relation to the so-called typical population.

These figure cannot help but make us question our social attitudes about perfection and wonder if there truly is a majority for whom all designs, goods, and services must be standardized. Until accident and illness cease to occur, until medicine and science achieve the ultimate miracle for all ages and conditions of the mortal realm, all the nondisabled are at times, and ultimately, the disabled.

Index

Page numbers in boldface type refer to illustrations.

125

About the Author

Jane Randolph Cary, a native of Virginia, attended Madison College in Harrisonburg and holds a B.S. degree from Columbia University. After seventeen years in retail merchandising and advertising, she moved into business and consumer publishing, where she now works as a free-lance writer and home building and furnishings editor. She is the recipient of a special citation from the Women's Auxiliary of the National Association of Home Builders (1971) and of the Burlington House Editorial Award (1972).